NOTTINGHAMSHIRE
FOLK TALES

NOTTINGHAMSHIRE

FOLK TALES

PETE CASTLE

The History Press

To disciples and followers of Robin Hood everywhere;
and to everyone who loves a good story.

First published 2012
Reprinted 2014, 2021

The History Press
97 St George's Place,
Cheltenham, Gloucestershire, GL50 3QB
www.thehistorypress.co.uk

British Library Cataloguing in Publication Data.
A catalogue record for this book is available from the British Library.

ISBN 978 0 7524 6377 3

Typesetting and origination by The History Press
Printed by TJ Books Limited, Padstow, Cornwall

CONTENTS

Acknowledgements

Thanks are due once again, to Sue who continues to put up with me both sitting at the computer and gallivanting off on singing and storytelling trips. She's also a fount of ideas and an indispensable critic and proof reader.

To Roy Harris, for the citation, various bits of information, and for being my mentor all those years ago.

To Stephen Best: man of Nottingham, friend, and source of advice and information on this subject.

To Lewis Brockway for the rear cover photo.

To Jenny Ball for the loan of books.

To the staff at both the Nottingham and Derbyshire (Matlock) local studies libraries for help with finding and copying material.

To all the many storytellers and folk musicians I've worked with over the years.

To all the many people who've sat in my audiences.

To you for buying this book.

INTRODUCTION

Old Mr Snotta built himself a hutta
By the side of the River Trent.
It was a very pleasant spot in the forest deep
And pretty soon he was collecting the rent.
Oh, the castle grew and the factories too
As the people came from miles around
To buy their food and sell their goods
In Mr Snotta's little town...

This is a dangerous task I attempt! Having already written *Derbyshire Folk Tales* in this series of county folk tales books for The History Press I am now going to attempt *Nottinghamshire Folk Tales*. The two cities (and, I suppose, the two counties) are great rivals. The only man who has been able to unite them in the recent past was Brian Clough via his achievements with Nottingham Forest and Derby County football clubs. Now the two cities are literally joined by the Brian Clough Way – the name given to the stretch of the A52 between the two cities. However, in the more distant past there were many other links – even the famous Sheriff of Nottingham was, in fact, the Sheriff of Nottingham and

Derby until Elizabethan times (therefore at the time of Robin Hood!) As you read these tales you will find other things the two counties have in common as well.

I'm not from Nottinghamshire. I was born a Man of Kent and I have lived in Derbyshire since 1987 but, back in the 1970s, I lived in Arnold, on the outskirts of Nottingham, for a few very influential years. For the last thirty-plus years I have worked professionally as a folk singer and storyteller, but without those few years spent in Nottingham my life would probably have taken a very different direction and I would not be writing this now, for it was during those years that I first began to take a serious interest in folk songs and folklore. I owe an awful lot to those years in Nottinghamshire.

I had discovered folk music whilst at college having played and sung in rock bands when I was at school, and I'd been toying around on the fringes of folk music – singing songs by Bob Dylan and Paul Simon as well as my own compositions (deeply influenced by the Incredible String Band) for several years by the time we moved to Arnold. In the 1970s, Nottinghamshire was one of the foremost areas in England for folk clubs and bands. (Several of the stories in this book gave rise to the names of clubs or groups—Bendigo's, Hemlock Stone etc.) We hadn't been in Nottingham long when I happened to go to a meeting which led to me starting a folk club in Arnold and then, a year or two later when it folded, I joined the committee of the very successful Carlton Folk Club which continued to run into the present century, long after I'd left. Whilst playing as a resident at Carlton I became more and more interested in traditional songs. I learned many and also wrote a few 'imitation' folk songs, the most successful of which was probably the Goose Fair

Song which was taken up, sung, and even recorded, by several other singers and groups.

Somehow my wife, Sue, and I also managed to get ourselves a series on Radio Nottingham called 'Sing a Song of Nottingham'. It was a series of five programmes, each with a theme – Sherwood Forest, Coal Mining, People… etc – built around mainly local songs which we performed. I wrote the little song at the top as the theme tune. I suspect the series might have been fairly bad and very naïve, but it sowed a lot of seeds for the kind of work which I've done since, including six years running a local radio folk programme after we'd left Nottingham and moved down to Bedfordshire. It was whilst in Bedfordshire that I took the major step of giving up my job as a teacher and going on the road full time as a professional folk musician. A few years later I discovered storytelling and have been doing the two, in tandem, ever since.

ABOUT NOTTINGHAMSHIRE FOLK TALES

When I wrote *Derbyshire Folk Tales* I had no trouble in finding stories from every part of the county, in fact Derby itself received but scant attention. I have found Nottinghamshire to be very different. Most of the stories look to Nottingham. Even if they are set elsewhere in the county, the participants are often going to or coming from the city. There are comparatively few stories which are rooted entirely in any of the other towns and villages. This is probably because until recently there were few other big settlements in the county. Newark and Southwell spring to mind but apart from those, there were only small market towns and hamlets scattered through the forest and, of course, the large estates of the nobility – the Dukeries. There are many stories about the gentry and nobility.

With its forests, its grand houses and its wide open spaces, Nottinghamshire, if it were on the Continent, would be an ideal setting for terrifying tales of wolves and vampires, evil Counts and little girls lost in the depths of the dark wood but, no, this is quiet, calm, middle England, where you are never far from the Great North Road and can soon escape to civilisation, so there are very few dark tales of that sort – although I have found some to include here.

In the eighteenth/nineteenth century, industry came to the county in the form of mining and factories. Tiny hamlets became pit villages which rose, and fell again when the pits closed in the 1980s, if not before. Nottingham became a manufacturing town but retained its literary and intellectual elite. I am well aware, and even feel slightly guilty, about the fact that I have not explored the folk tales of the mines and factories. I know there are a lot of customs and superstitions connected with both and I think there must be stories too, but it is a whole different world which I would have to explore and I haven't had the time – perhaps that's another book? Meanwhile, those traditions survive in songs and in the novels of writers as diverse as D.H. Lawrence and Alan Sillitoe.

There are a lot of what could be called 'true stories' in this collection – stories about people who have actually existed. How much of their stories actually happened though, is a different matter – they are collected from bits of gossip, tall tales, and legends. Whether Robin Hood fits into this category is open to discussion and is a matter of personal belief.

ABOUT STORIES AND STORYTELLING

This is not a book of stories I've created, and it is not a history book. Most of the stories in this book are traditional, and even where I have mentioned a source – a publisher or a book – that is usually the man who collected or published the story, not the man (or woman) who 'made it up', for they are folk tales and they are, by definition, anonymous. This book is a miscellany, a hotchpotch, a cornucopia of different sorts of stories from different sources. They come from all periods of history and all classes of people. You will find fairy tales, legends, tall tales, bits of gossip, jokes, and retellings of historical events. You won't find real, accurate history. Where the events actually happened, or where the characters actually lived, it is the *story* which has been told, not the facts.

Folk tales inhabit a world of contradictions: on the one hand, they take an event and blow it up out of all proportion, then pass it on in a form in which it could not possibly have happened, and once the story has taken root it proves almost impossible for a historian to say, 'No, it couldn't have happened like that'. People's reaction is to say that it did in the story so it must have! A quote I am fond of using to sum this up is, 'When the legend becomes fact print the legend' (words spoken by the journalist at the end of John Ford's film *The Man Who Shot Liberty Valence*). But that determination to remain unchanged also means that folk tales sometimes preserve, over thousands of years, information that has long been forgotten by scholars. Studying folk tales can almost be like archaeology; sometimes you can excavate a small gem of truth from a lot of rubble.

Most of these tales have existed in an oral form at one time or another. They were probably passed on by word of mouth for many years, perhaps, even, for many generations before they were written down. That is the case with all kinds of folklore – it moves from the mouth to the page and then back to the mouth, and each form influences the other.

I am a story *teller*. I was telling stories for decades before I was asked to write any down. Writing is a different art form to telling – you cannot successfully transcribe a story as it is told. Telling a story in a live situation involves using gesture and tone of voice, something which does not come across when it is written. Also, a live telling is told in a particular environment which can colour the telling; one of the reasons it is really enjoyable to tell a story in the place where it is supposed to have happened.

I started off trying to group the stories here like I did in the Derbyshire book, but they didn't fit into sections like that so I thought I wouldn't group them at all, I'd just let them run on from one to another – a 'chain' of stories, like I might do when telling them live. In a live telling you add introductions, say why you like the story and what it means to you – in other words, add a bit of yourself to the story. I have done that here. When I had finished the arrangement of stories I found that, rather than a random selection, they had actually grouped themselves, but under very different headings to the ones I had intended. Stories are like that, they have minds of their own!

The other big difference between the two books is, of course, the illustrations. For the Derbyshire book I asked an old friend, Ray Aspden, to do them, but when we were nearly finished I found myself asking 'why didn't I do them myself?' When I was a boy I was always 'good at drawing', and my education took the path it did largely for that reason. I was going to do something to do with 'art' when I grew up. As it happened I ended up teaching in primary schools, although my main study at college had been art. Although I can draw, I've found that I can't paint. After college I had a ceremonial burning of all my work and decided I wouldn't do any more. I tried to paint again for a short time in the 1980s but was never happy with the results. I preferred songs and stories. However, I can still draw and I've really enjoyed getting back to some serious artwork for this book. I had to work at it but I hope you like them too.

The brief for this whole series of books is that they are folk tales, retold by working oral storytellers and we've all had to walk the line between the two art forms – story *telling* and story *writing*. I want the stories to work in the book, but I also want them to have the immediacy and informality of an oral telling. I would like nothing better than, in a few years time, to come across you telling a story and to realise that it was one you came across here. I would count that a huge compliment. They are stories for telling; please tell them.

Pete Castle, Belper, 2012

For more info please visit:
www.petecastle.co.uk and www.factsandfiction.co.uk

ONE

THE WISE MEN OF GOTHAM

Three wise men of Gotham
Went to sea in a bowl;
If the bowl had been stronger
My tale would have been longer.

It seems fitting to start this collection of Nottinghamshire stories with a smaller collection of stories, a collection of tales which might well be the oldest ones in this book, the tales of the 'Wise Men of Gotham'. Most, if not all, of these stories had been circulating orally for several centuries before they were published in 1540 in a pamphlet entitled 'The Merry Tales of the Mad Men of Gotham', by a writer using the pseudonym A.B. of Phisicke Doctor. His booklet contained twenty tales about the exploits of the inhabitants of this small village, which lies just a few miles south-west of Nottingham. The pamphlet remained in print into the nineteenth century and some of the stories are still amongst the best known of all Nottinghamshire, even British, folk tales. It's hard to find a collection in which one or two don't crop up. The tales were so well known in America, that Washington Irving used Gotham as a satirical name for New York City, and DC Comics continued that idea with the name for the city where Batman lived.

So, for centuries the 'Wise Men of Gotham' (or the Gotham Fools) has been a byword for stupid, silly, or eccentric behaviour. Other people from other places have done strange things too, but you can be pretty sure that the men of Gotham did it first or better. For example, the famous Wiltshire story of the moonrakers actually began with the Gothamites. Here follows a selection of their other doings.

THE MEN OF GOTHAM AND THE CUCKOO

The men of Gotham noticed that the arrival of the cuckoo was a sign that summer was on its way. So, they put their heads together and used their formidable intelligence to come up with a plan that might prevent the cuckoo from flying away again. They thought that if the cuckoo stayed all year then summer might stay all year too. A good idea! They waited until a cuckoo landed in a tree in the middle of the village, and then they quickly built a high wooden fence around it. But when it wanted to leave the cuckoo just flew over it, of course. 'Oh dear,' lamented the men of Gotham, 'we didn't build it high enough. Next year . . . '

This is, quite possibly, the best known Gotham story and is celebrated by the sign on the village pub: The Cuckoo Bush.

THE MEN OF GOTHAM DROWN AN EEL

In the old days, Lent was a time of strict fasting and everyone solemnly kept to the diet that the Church prescribed: no meat, no eggs, no fat and so on. The main food they ate during Lent was fish: salted fish, dried fish, white herrings, red herrings, kippers and all kinds of fish.

On Good Friday, when the fast was over, the men of Gotham got together to decide what to do with the spare fish they had not eaten. They decided that the best thing to do was to throw them into the pond so that they could breed again, ready for next year. So that is what they did.

The following year, when Lent approached, the men all went to the pond to catch a new supply of fish but all they could catch was a large, fat eel. 'He's eaten all our fish,' they cried. 'We must punish him. What shall we do with him?'

They suggested all kinds of punishments but the one they liked best was to drown him. So they threw him back into the pond.

THE MEN OF GOTHAM AND THE SHEEP

A man from Gotham was going to Nottingham to buy sheep. He arrived at a bridge just as another man from Gotham, who was coming from Nottingham, arrived at the other end of the bridge. 'Where are you going?' asked the one coming from Nottingham.

'I'm going to Nottingham to buy sheep,' came the reply.

'And which way will you bring them back?'

'Why, I'll drive them across this bridge, of course.'

'Oh no you won't!'

'Oh yes I will, and if you don't let me drive them cross the bridge then they'll jump over the stream.'

And the two men started to act out driving the imaginary sheep. One man herded them across the bridge and the other waved his arms to stop them and send them back the way they'd come.

Soon, a third man of Gotham came along carrying a sack of meal from the mill. He stopped and watched the two men herding invisible sheep and then asked them what they were doing. When they told him he thought for a minute and then emptied his sack into the river. 'Now tell me,' he said, 'how much meal is there in this sack?'

They told him there was none, the sack was empty.

'Well then,' he said, 'there's just as much meal in this sack as there are brains in your heads.'

He had taught them a lesson, but at what cost?

Which of these men of Gotham was the wisest or, for that matter, the silliest?

THE MEN OF GOTHAM AND THE CHEESE

A man from Gotham was on his way to the market in Nottingham to sell his cheeses. As he was going down a hill he dropped a cheese and, being shaped like a wheel, it rolled off in front of him. 'Oh, so you know the way to Nottingham, do you?' he said. 'Well, if you do I suppose the others do too.' So, he took the other cheeses out of his bag and rolled them down the hill. 'Off you go to Nottingham,' he said, 'and wait for me at the market.'

As he walked on his way he thought to himself that this was much easier than carrying the cheeses and he wondered why he hadn't thought of it before.

Soon he came to Nottingham and went into the Market Square to find his cheeses, but they were nowhere to be seen. He asked around but no one had seen them, so he waited and waited until the day drew to a close and the market closed, yet still no cheeses had arrived.

'Oh,' he thought, 'they must have misunderstood me and not stopped in Nottingham. I bet they're half way to York by now.' So he borrowed a horse and set off to York to find them. But he never did!

THE MAN OF GOTHAM AND HIS HORSE

One day, a man from Gotham was going to market to sell two big bundles of faggots. They were too heavy for him to carry so he first thought of tying them onto his horse, but then he would have to walk and he wanted to ride because it was quite a long way. He didn't think it was fair for the horse to have to carry both him and the faggots so he wondered how he could lighten the load. Inspiration! The horse could carry him and he would carry the faggots. He mounted the horse and tied the bundles of faggots round his own neck so that the load was fairly split between them.

THE MEN OF GOTHAM AND THE HARE

It was rent day and the men of Gotham had forgotten to pay their landlords. They were worried because if it wasn't paid that day then they could all be fined or even evicted. Then one of them had an idea. That very day he had caught a hare. 'A hare is a very quick animal,' he said. 'He can run much faster than we can. Why don't we give it to him to take to our lords?' The others thought that this was a good idea, so they wrote a letter explaining what had happened and put it, with the money, into a purse and tied it round the hare's neck. Then they very carefully explained to the hare where he had to go and which was the best route to take. 'First you go to Lancaster,' they said, 'and then to Loughborough, and then you finish up at Newark,' for their various landlords were in those places.

As soon as the hare was free it rushed off across the field in entirely the wrong direction. 'You've got to go to Lancaster first . . . ,' someone yelled. 'Don't worry,' said the others, 'he probably knows a much quicker route.'

THE MEN OF GOTHAM AND THE CANDLE

One day, four men from Gotham decided to sit silently and gaze at a candle without speaking for a week. Why? I have no idea! Just as evening fell on the first day the candle flickered and went out. The first man said, 'Oh! The candle has gone out.' The second man said, 'Shhh! we're not supposed to talk!' The third man said, 'Be quiet, you two!' The fourth man laughed and said, 'Ha! I'm the only one who hasn't spoken.' But, of course, by that point he had.

THE MEN OF GOTHAM CROSS A RIVER

Here is an additional tale which didn't, when I first heard it, apply to the men of Gotham; although there is one about them crossing a river. This was told to me by Punjabi story-teller Peter Chand, who called it 'The Seven Silly Fakirs' and it included crocodiles, of which there are none in the River

Trent, so I have changed it a bit. It illustrates how stories of
fools are world wide – unless Peter, or someone before him,
took a Gotham story and transported it to India, of course.
In which case, it's gone full circle.

Seven men from Gotham were out walking in the countryside when they found their way blocked by a wide river.
There seemed no option but to wade across, even though
it was deep and fast-flowing. They were terrified that they
would get swept away and drowned but they said their
prayers and waded into the water. They made their way
across to the other side, where they clambered up the bank
in various different places, dripping with water, and with
much puffing and blowing and spluttering. When they
were all assembled they started to check they had all made it
safely across. One man counted, starting from the man on
his left and going round the circle until he reached the man
on his right: 1… 2… 3… 4… 5… 6…

'There are only six of us,' he sobbed. 'One of us has drowned.'

'No, you haven't counted right, let me do it,' said another
and did the same thing: 1… 2… 3… 4… 5… 6… He got
the same answer.

Then all of them, in turn, had a try and all of them came up with the same number, six, but they could not decide who was missing.

'It's the blacksmith, he's not here.'

'Yes I am. It must be the baker.'

'No, it's not me, I'm here.'

They argued and worried for a while, trying to figure out which of them was missing for, as you have no doubt realised, these silly men had all forgotten to include themselves when counting. Just then, a stranger came by and heard all the fuss.

'What are you all arguing about?' he asked. When they explained he burst out laughing.

'There are none of you missing,' he said, 'you all crossed the river safely and I'll prove it to you. Look, here is a nice juicy cowpat. Kneel down round it and poke your noses into the pat, then all we need do is count the holes and we'll know how many of you there are.'

So the seven silly men of Gotham knelt down and poked their noses into the cowpat. Then they stood up and counted the holes. 1... 2... 3... 4... 5... 6... 7! They all agreed there were seven nose holes; none of them had been drowned.

And the seven silly men of Gotham went happily on their way, arm-in-arm, each with a little blob of cow dung on his nose.

THE WOMEN OF GOTHAM

It was not just the men of Gotham who behaved strangely, and for the sake of equality I have made room here for at least one tale about their wives.

One day, the women of Gotham were sat in the tavern discussing their attributes and talents and trying to decide which of their husbands had got the best deal when they married.

The first woman said that she couldn't be beaten for reliability. Every day she did the same thing in exactly the same way so she was the most reliable. And what did she do? Nothing!

The second said that her great talent was frugality. She saved her husband a fortune in candles. How? Every day, whether winter or summer, she and her family stopped work and went to bed whilst it was still light, so they never needed to light a candle.

The third said that she saved her husband money by hardly eating anything at all. She didn't really care for bread or meat so she ate very little of it. She lived purely by drinking. But she did drink a gallon of ale every day.

The fourth wife said that she did even better; she saved money by never drinking at home. She spent all her time in the tavern where she ate and drank anything that anyone would give her.

The fifth wife made sure she did not bore her husband. In order to ensure this she divided her time equally between him and several other men.

The sixth said that she made sure she didn't wear out her furniture by spending all her time visiting other people in their houses.

Number seven did something similar; she spent every day sat before other people's fires so she and her husband never ran out of firewood.

The eighth wife said that pork, mutton and chicken were too expensive for her to buy so, instead, she bought the meat of pigs, sheep and fowls.

The ninth wife saved her husband the money most women spent on soap because instead of doing the washing once a week she only washed once a quarter.

The ale wife, who owned the tavern where they were gathered, spoke last. She said that she saved her husband more money than all the rest of them because, whereas she used to like to drink a drop of his ale, she now drank it all and so prevented it from going sour and wasting.

It is not recorded which of them was voted to be the best wife, but you can make up your own mind.

THE MEN OF GOTHAM: THE TRUTH (ALLEGEDLY)

Why should the men of Gotham (and the women for that matter) have gained such a reputation for stupidity? Is there any truth in it? Did any of it really happen? Or was it some kind of clever plot?

Well, there is a theory (or it may be just another story) that it was all play acting, that they deliberately set out to make it appear that the village was inhabited by simpletons; and for good reason. It all goes back to the time of King John, who gets blamed for many things.

King John was travelling to Nottingham to stay in the castle there and it became obvious that his route would take him through the village of Gotham. Now, the people in the village did not fancy the King and his retinue of several hundred greedy courtiers passing through the village, taking away everything they owned in the way of food and provisions. They knew that it would be like an army of locusts passing through and they'd be left with nothing. So how were they going to prevent it? They could hardly take up arms and build barricades, physically preventing the King from travelling that way; they had to be far more subtle about it. They knew that the King would send scouts in advance to check on the route and to plan resting and eating places, so they arranged that when the scouts arrived at Gotham they would find the people behaving so strangely that they would recommend that the King should avoid the place. They played their parts so well that everybody, not just the King, believed the story, and it has been preserved to this day.

Variations on the theme are that any road the King passed along automatically became a public highway and they did not want a public road through the village with all the upkeep that would entail; or that the King was planning to build a hunting lodge in the vicinity, which they did not want either.

TWO

STORIES ABOUT GOOSE FAIR

Several of the Men of Gotham stories mention going to market. Markets sometimes developed into fairs. The most notable fair in Nottinghamshire is, obviously, Nottingham's Goose Fair. Goose Fair is one of the largest fairs in England (Newcastle, Hull and Nottingham dispute which is actually the largest, it depends on how you measure it: by area covered, by money taken, or what). Anyway, it has been one of the major events in the Nottingham calendar for centuries. It started over 700 years ago. Nowadays it is a huge funfair held on the Forest Recreation Ground. Previously it had been held in the Market Square (or 'Slab Square' as the locals call it) until the rides and machines outgrew that space. Now it is entirely a funfair, but it had its roots in a market where geese were sold. Breeders would herd their flocks of geese from as far away as Lincolnshire and Norfolk, making their way slowly along the roads grazing as they went (often with shoes made of tar on their feet to protect them). They would enter Nottingham through Goosegate and make their way to the Market Square. The word gate in that, and other Nottingham street names, doesn't mean a gate as we picture it – not a farmer's five-bar gate – it is derived from the Viking word 'gata', meaning street. The geese were intended for the traditional Michaelmas feast on 29 September, although Goose Fair is now held in the first week of October.

There are several stories about how and why the fair began, which are far more interesting than the factual account above. Here is my favourite.

HOW GOOSE FAIR BEGAN

One day, a man was fishing in the River Trent. He felt a tug on his line and, as was the way in those days, when people were fishing for food not for sport, he immediately gave the rod a huge pull, aiming to heave the fish out of the water and onto the bank in one go: no playing with it and tiring it out.

The fish, a large pike, flew up into the air just at the exact moment a goose was flying overhead. Seeing the fish so close, the goose automatically seized it in its beak and flew on. But, the pike was connected to the hook and the hook was connected to the line, the line was connected to the rod and the rod was held firmly by the fisherman who was not going to lose his fish. So, pulling pike, rod, line and fisherman behind it the goose flew on until it was over the Market Square, where it sank to the ground in exhaustion.

The fisherman was amazed to land on the ground unscathed and was so pleased that he pronounced that the day was to be an annual holiday and the townsfolk held a fair to celebrate it. And, although they've forgotten what it is they are celebrating, they continue to celebrate with style, as the next two stories show.

THE YOUNG MAN'S FIRST VISIT
TO GOOSE FAIR

There was, in Nottingham, a certain gentleman who had had a very bad experience of married life. His courtship had been difficult, as had the first years of their marriage and, soon after their son was born, his wife left him. The gentleman then vowed that his son would not be put through so much sorrow and that he would bring him up ignorant to the wiles of women; in fact he'd have no contact with them at all. Somehow, he managed to achieve this and the son reached adolescence without ever having met, or even seen, a woman. He was ignorant of their very existence.

The father now decided that, his son having become a young man, he should introduce him to more of the world's experiences, so he decided to take him to Goose Fair to see the acrobats and the jugglers; the wild animals and the freaks; to taste the foods and to enjoy the rides. He still hoped, however, to keep the young man ignorant of women.

The boy enjoyed the fair and all the new sights and sounds and experiences. At last, he seemed to be very taken with a broad straw hat and the feather in it and, more than anything, with the face below it. 'What's that, Father?' he asked.

'A goose, nothing but a silly goose,' replied his father. And then the boy noticed more and more of these exotic creatures walking arm-in-arm and giggling and laughing, and once again he asked what they were. 'I told you,' said the father, 'they are nothing but silly geese.'

At the end of the evening the father took his son to one side and explained that it was time to go home and that it was traditional to take a present, a 'fairing', home to remind you of the good time you'd had at the fair. He asked his son what he would like to have. Without a moment's hesitation the boy said, 'Why, Father, that's easy. A goose, nothing but a silly goose.'

THE BACHELORS OF DERBY GO TO GOOSE FAIR

This story comes from an old ballad, not a ballad which could be sung but a poem in ballad form, and was included by Llewellyn Jewitt in his book *The Ballads and Songs of Derbyshire*. Jewitt's title was: 'The Unconsionable Batchelors of Darby: Or the Young Lasses Pawn'd by their Sweet-hearts, for a large Reckning, at Nottingham Goose Fair, where poor Susan was forced to pay the Shot'. It's a timeless piece of nonsense about how lads trick girls, and how girls fall for the lad's tricks. It could have happened two hundred years ago; it could have happened last year; it could happen next year.

It was Goose Fair time and many of the young men and women of Derby were preparing to go, as they did every year. Most of them went in groups, sometimes groups of men, sometimes groups of women, but sometimes, and that was the best, in mixed groups. Kate and Sue were going with several young men of their acquaintance. For weeks before, the young men had been vying for the honour of accompanying the two young women and boasting about how they would treat them and what a good time they would give them. Kate and Sue were sure that they would have a really enjoyable day, and perhaps even manage to catch a husband, which, at the time, is what all the young women of their age and class were trying to do. The men were not necessarily aiming at marriage but they were hoping to get as intimate as possible with the young women.

When the day came the whole group met in Derby and caught the coach which would carry them the fifteen miles or so down the turnpike to Nottingham.

When they reached the fairground the young men bowed low and welcomed the girls, inviting them to join them in the refreshment tent. Kate and Sue thought they were going to be treated to all kinds of luxuries so willingly accompanied them. The young men acted like perfect gentlemen and ordered cakes, ale, cider, mead and anything else which took the girls' fancy. They complimented them and flirted in a harmless fashion. Kate, who was a beauty and knew well how to keep the young men interested, fluttered her eyelids and played hard to get. She and Sue knew what it was they wanted to win at the fair and so they played the young men at their own game. However, in the end, it was the girls who found themselves cheated, for all of a sudden the young men took their leave and swiftly left the refreshment tent.

Sue and Kate found themselves alone with a table full of empty glasses and memories of empty promises. They reassured themselves by ordering another round of drinks and more cakes, and they told each other that the men had just gone off to buy them some fairings; souvenirs of a lovely day at the fair. They wondered what they would both be given when the men returned, and they discussed the merits of the various young men and which of them would be the best catch.

The time passed and the young men did not return for they had sneaked away, leaving Sue and Kate to pay the bill for all the refreshments the men had so gallantly ordered. When it became clear that the men were not coming back the girls called for the bill and to their horror discovered that it amounted to 15 shillings. Kate had only 5 pence in her purse – she had been depending on the men's generosity – but luckily Sue had a guinea. When the bill had been paid Kate and Sue were in no mood for enjoying the fair any more so they caught the coach home to Derby. On the way, they complained that it had cost them all their money and they had not even managed to win one kiss.

So, the young women of Derby, who had hoped to have a good time at the expense of the young men, found the boot on the other foot.

OLD JACKEY PEET: THE GREEDIEST MAN IN NOTTINGHAM

I first came across the story of Jackey Peet back in the early 1970s, when I lived in Nottingham, and I wrote a song about him. When I came to compile this collection, I wanted to find out more about him but couldn't track him down until I was leant an old book, *Briscoe's Stories of the Midlands*, published in 1883, and there he was, rubbing shoulders with members of the aristocracy. He seems to have been born around 1768.

Jackey Peet was a young man who lived in the middle of Nottingham, back when it was still quite a small town. His family was poor and they lived in a poor house in a very poor part of the town. Jackey had three main interests: flowers, decorating his clothing and, above all, food. It was food which brought about his downfall, but we'll come back to that in a minute.

Many people like flowers and some wear a bloom in their buttonholes. Jackey Peet was not content with a single bloom or even two – he would, if he could, attach a whole bouquet of flowers to his jacket. He also wore a large 'brooch', which was a lion's head and was originally intended to be attached to a piece of furniture. And then there were his buttons and brooches. He collected them whenever he could and his jacket and shirt front were adorned with a collection of different buttons of different sizes in different materials. People who wanted to tease him would ask for a button, or threaten to take one, and it always threw Jackey into great paroxysms of fear or rage.

Jackey would, grudgingly, do work if he had to, or run errands for his mother, but if the faintest chance of food arose he would forget whatever it was he was supposed to be doing and hunt it down like the keenest of bloodhounds.

Because of this love of food Jackey grew bigger and bigger. As he grew older he obviously grew taller as all young men do, but Jackey grew broader too. Soon he was nearly as wide as he was tall and the distance round his waist was much more than the distance between his outstretched fingertips.

Jackey couldn't sleep in a bed because none was strong enough to take his weight, but he didn't mind sleeping on the floor. He couldn't sit in a chair because the legs were never strong enough. There was no way Jackey could have ridden on a horse or in a wagon, but that didn't matter because his family couldn't afford to use them anyway. If Jackey had to go anywhere he walked.

Because of his size and because he was, in the language of the day, a bit 'simple', Jackey became well known all over Nottingham. People loved to see him eat. They would produce huge quantities of food just to see how much he could manage – a whole plum pudding followed by a bucketful of broth for instance, and some cruel people dared him to eat all kinds of strange things; which he usually did. He always entered the pie-eating contests which they held at Goose Fair, and he always won! His proudest possession was the medal he was awarded one year. He wore it on his chest and would show it to everyone he met. His mother loved him dearly and was proud of him and his exploits in a strange way, but she told the tale that even when he was a baby she couldn't cope with his appetite so she had to put him to a wet nurse and he'd drunk the wet nurse dry!

He continued to be a great drinker and in later life his favourite ditty was:

Come unto my nose;

Ale, good ale;

And down it goes!

One day, around Goose Fair time, Jackey had an amazing piece of luck, or so it seemed to him at the time. As he was mooching around the alleyways in the town doing nothing and going nowhere in particular, he smelled the unmistakable aroma of freshly cooked meat. His nose, honed by years of practice, led him to what seemed a blank wall, no food anywhere in sight. But Jackey knew that the mouth-watering smell must be coming from somewhere near. He searched all around and then he found a crack in the wall. He poked his finger in and dislodged a tiny piece of hard, brittle earth (the walls in that part of town were all built of wattle and daub) and once he had removed a small piece he could put in two fingers and remove a larger piece; the bigger the hole became, the easier it was to knock out more and more of the filling between the wooden framework. Soon, Jackey had made a hole big enough to put his head through and he could see that there was a pantry on the other side of the wall. What could be better! The mouth-watering smell was coming from a large leg of meat which was still steaming on a platter. There were also pies and pastries and loaves of bread. Hanging from hooks in the ceiling were hams and sides of bacon. In tubs on the floor were apples and dried fruits. It was Jackey Peet's idea of heaven.

He worked as quickly and quietly as he could to make the hole even larger and soon he was able, with a great deal of difficulty, to squeeze his way in. Once in, he didn't waste a minute. He started eating and didn't stop until the pantry was empty. Then he fell asleep. It's a wonder that the rumbles and grumblings of his stomach didn't wake the whole neighbourhood, but no one heard a thing – perhaps they were all at the fair.

A few hours later, Jackey was woken by the sound of doors banging and the bustle of people coming into the house. The owners had come home and were now ready for a good meal. He'd better make a quick getaway, he thought. But Jackey had eaten so much that he'd grown even bigger round the waist and, try as he might, he could not get back out of the hole he'd got in by. He tried to make it larger but there was the strong wooden framework which supported the wall and about which he could do nothing. Try as he might there was no escape. Jackey Peet was trapped. In the end he had to give up and admit that he was caught.

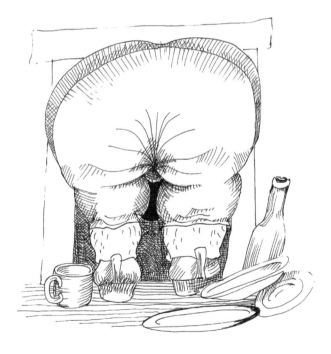

When the housewife came in to get the food for their meal pandemonium broke loose. She screamed, her husband roared, the constable was called; all the neighbours rushed in and beat Jackey with anything they could lay their hands on. Eventually he was taken and put in the stocks in the Market Place where, insult of insults, the townsfolk threw food at him.

After that Jackey Peet was more careful. He still ate everything he could get his hands on but he made sure that he was not caught stealing food again.

Word of his escapade spread through the town and Jackey became the butt of many jokes and tricks. Years later someone even commemorated his adventure in a song:

> Old Jackey Peet you must be
> The greediest man in Nottingham.
> Old Jackey Peet you might even be
> The greediest man in the whole country.

THREE

NOTTINGHAM FIGHTERS

BENDIGO THE BOXER

This is another true story, which shows that the 'professional foul' is not a recent invention of continental footballers and that some sportsmen have built a whole career on it. It's about another, real-life, Nottingham character.

> You didn't know of Bendigo?
> Well that knocks me out!
> Who's your board schoolteacher?
> What's he been about?
> Chock a block with fairy tales;
> Full of useless cram,
> And never heard of Bendigo
> The Pride Of Nottingham.
> (from *Bendigo's Sermon* by Sir Arthur Conan Doyle)

Bendigo, Bendy, or, as he was officially christened, William Abednego Thompson, was, for many years in the mid-

1800s, the most famous bare-knuckle boxer, or prize fighter, in England. He was born in 1811 in the poor streets, between Long Row and Parliament Street, in the centre of Nottingham – much the same area in which Jackey Peet lived. It was a large family; he was one of triplets and there were eighteen other children before them. When she realised that she had given birth to three babies, their mother called them Shadrach, Meshak and Abednego – after the three young men in the Bible story who were thrown into a burning fiery furnace in Babylon, but came out unharmed. Perhaps the names were a good omen because Bendigo proved to be a survivor too.

From an early age Bendigo was good at sports and good at looking after himself. He had to be because his father had died when he was fifteen years old, and he and his mother spent time in the workhouse. Then he sold oysters around the streets before getting a job as an iron turner. Menial jobs like that are hard work and poorly paid and Bendigo kept his eyes open for easier ways of making money. Prize fighting seemed to be one of these, providing you won and didn't mind getting hurt in the process; he didn't. Although he wasn't the biggest fighter around he was quick and agile and often made his opponents look stupid and clumsy. Like Cassius Clay a century later, he was an entertainer as well as a fighter; he made up rhymes about his opponents and taunted them; he insulted their mothers and pulled faces; wound up the crowd and generally made the other fighters so angry that they'd lost the fight before it even started. But, if the fighters hated him the crowds loved him and he could soon entice thousands of fans out to the remote fields or barns where bare-knuckle fights took place in those days.

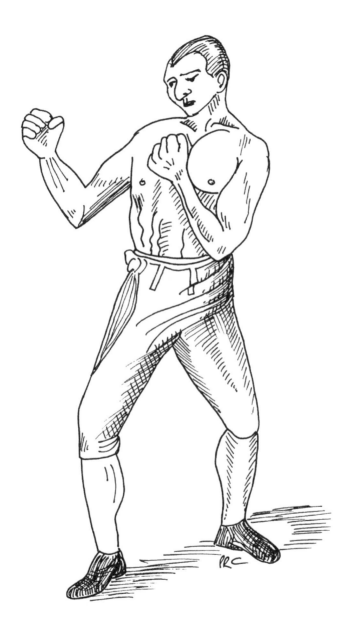

At this point it might be useful to consider the rules for prize fighting. These rules were laid out by Jack Broughton, a famous fighter, in 1743.

The sport was illegal so it usually happened in out-of-the-way places where the authorities would not turn up unannounced. Although, if 15,000 spectators knew where to go I don't see that they couldn't have gone too – if they had dared!

Fights took place in a defined space – you weren't allowed to run away – although the size of that space was not stipulated.

In the middle of that space was a square yard. The fighters had to face each other at opposite sides of this square after each break.

Each fighter had a second to look after him.

The fighters fought for a purse, of which the winner received two-thirds.

A round lasted until a fighter was knocked down. Then he was allowed thirty seconds to be ready to start again. If he wasn't, he lost the fight.

A fighter on his knees was deemed 'down'.

Going down without being hit, just to have a rest, could lead to disqualification.

Strangling, kicking and so on were illegal but often used. Certain throws were allowed.

These were the rules in force until John Douglas, the 9th Marquess of Queensbury, laid out the rules for present-day boxing in 1867.

Now, every hero needs a villain. Cassius Clay had Sonny Liston; Bendigo had Ben Caunt. Caunt, the 'Torkard Giant', was another Nottinghamshire man, from Hucknall, and they fought each other several times over the years.

Bendigo should have lost his first fight against Caunt, but if he had then he wouldn't have entered into Nottinghamshire folklore and I wouldn't be telling this story. He was out-classed by the bigger, heavier man and was having difficulty in staying on his feet. He resorted to trickery – to dancing, to pulling faces, to maniacal giggling. In the end, it was too much for Caunt, who lost his temper and hit Bendigo when he was down on one knee, a foul. So Caunt was disqualified and Bendigo was declared the winner. The fight had lasted twenty-two rounds, quite short for those days. His next two fights lasted for fifty-two and fifty-one rounds respectively.

And then came Looney. William Looney from Liverpool placed a letter in a newspaper challenging 'any man in the world for a £200 stake and £200 a-side'. The fight took place on 13 June 1837, on a hill at Chapel-en-le-Frith, the half-way point between their home towns. This fight lasted for a massive ninety-two rounds. The highlight came in the fif-teenth round when Bendigo saw Looney winding up for a haymaker. He threw himself backwards onto his shoulders, waved his legs in the air and roared with laughter. After that he took control of the fight and entertained the crowd with all his tricks, although it nearly went wrong when Looney caught him with a lucky punch late on.

The following year, Bendigo had a rematch with Caunt. Both fighters were desperate to win 'by any means necessary' and it degenerated into a riot with both sets of supporters involved. Caunt was rescued by his seconds and attempted to escape in a coach but it was held up by Bendigo's fans, and he only escaped by riding off bareback on a stolen horse.

Bendigo's finest achievement came in 1839 when he defeated the Londoner, James 'Deaf un' Burke, for the All

England title and a purse of 200 guineas (a fortune in those days) in front of a crowd of 15,000. For a title fight it was a disappointment though – Bendigo won in a mere ten rounds after goading Burke into head-butting him; resulting in him being disqualified for the act.

William 'Bendigo' Thompson, 'The Nottingham Jester', 'Champion Prize Fighter of All England' was presented with his Champion's Belt a few weeks later, at the Queens Theatre, Liverpool. When he got home to Nottingham he met his supporters and, in the excitement, somersaulted off the stage into the crowd, crashed to the floor and broke his kneecap. This stopped him fighting for the next two years and he never quite regained his earlier agility.

Once his knee was healed Bendigo fought nineteen fights in the next four years and then came the final showdown with Caunt. It was one of the dirtiest fights ever. Most of the supporters came to finish the business they'd started at the previous meeting. It made the worst local derby football match look tame. The fighters used every dirty trick and foul in the book, and many that weren't, and Bendigo deliberately wore down and humiliated Caunt round by round until, in round number ninety-six, Caunt just sat down and refused to continue, thus forfeiting the fight.

Bendigo only fought one more fight. For the next few years he took to the much quieter pastime of fishing and won several All England titles at that sport too.

But then, in 1850, came a challenge from Tom Paddock of Redditch. It was like the typical western film plot – the old gunfighter wanting to hang up his guns and retire gracefully, the young upstarts wanting to make a name for themselves by facing him. Bendigo was quite willing to refuse the fight, to say he'd retired, but his mother would not let him. She called him a coward and said, 'If you won't fight him then I will!' (She was eighty-two!) It was the old story once again. Bendigo beat the younger, better fighter by tricking him into a foul in the forty-ninth round. And then Bendigo really did retire and took up the position of unofficial boxing coach at Cambridge University.

Now, all good folk tales tend to go in circles if they don't end with a 'happily ever after'. This tale is of the former in nature. Bendigo had started life as one of the poorest people in the poorest quarters of Nottingham. After his success in London, he returned to Nottingham and took to drink. He'd earned a lot of money from his fights but had never looked after it, and he now drank what remained away. The children in the streets teased and taunted the helpless drunk. He also became involved with the 'Nottingham Lambs', a gang of politically motivated hooligans who protested against the bad conditions in which people were forced to live, but they did so by rioting. It was this gang who burned down the castle.

As he spiralled into poverty and drunkenness, Bendigo moved to Beeston and took to religion. He became a popular preacher and used all his charisma and the tricks of working a crowd, which he had honed in his fighting days, to spread the word of God. For a while he toured the country.

Bendigo died on 23 August 1880, aged sixty-nine, after falling down the stairs in his home. The fall broke ribs which punctured his lung. His funeral was a grand affair with a procession over a mile long, including many national celebrities. Crowds lined the streets. He was buried with his mother in Bath Street Cemetery, now St Mary's Rest Gardens, where his memorial, a crouching lion, can still be seen.

FIGHTING NOBLEMEN: JACK MUSTERS AND SIR THOMAS PARKYNS

JACK MUSTERS: A century before Bendigo, another famous practitioner of 'the noble art' was Jack Musters, the squire of Annesley Hall. He was renowned as the best boxer, the best jumper and the best dancer in the whole of Nottinghamshire. But he had a rival in the field of boxing. The rival was a chimney sweep from Nottingham, who was sure he could beat Jack Musters. A proper match was never going to happen, because a gentleman would not be matched against a mere chimney sweep. The sweep put his mind to how he could arrange a meeting and came up with a clever idea. One day, he took his fishing rod, went to Annesley Hall, and sat himself down beside the squire's private fishing lake, where he could not fail to be seen. Musters happened to look out of the window and saw the sweep with his rod and line, so he flung on his coat, took his horse whip and confronted him. As Musters raised the whip, to teach the sweep a lesson for his impertinence, the sweep let fly a straight left which knocked him to the ground. Musters smiled; unhurt he climbed to his feet, flung down the whip, threw off his coat and faced up to the sweep. The fight lasted for two hours and, in the end, the sweep was victorious – he had knocked the squire unconscious. When Musters regained his senses they shook hands and the squire congratulated the victor. Then he took him into the house where he was given a glass of wine and told that he could fish in the lake whenever he wished.

BUNNY HALL

SIR THOMAS PARKYNS: Boxers were not the only fighters to be bred in Nottingham. Sir Thomas Parkyns was known as 'the wrestling baronet of Bunny Hall'. Bunny is a small village on the A60 Loughborough Road, south of Nottingham. Sir Thomas loved wrestling and had a permanent ring erected in the grounds. Fighters from all over the county were invited to participate and the bouts were arranged by drawing lots. The winner's names would be put back into the hat for the next round. Sir Thomas and several of his staff always competed and, surprisingly, Sir Thomas did not always win. The overall winner would be presented with 'a gold-laced hat value 2 guineas' and the runner-up would get 3 shillings.

Parkyns was such an enthusiast that he did not always keep his moves for official matches. There is a story that one day he was being visited by another nobleman and as they were walking through the grounds of Bunny Hall the conversation turned to wrestling. Probably just out of politeness the visitor said that he hoped to see Parkyns in action one day.

Without more ado Parkyns seized the visitor and threw him to the ground. When the visitor complained, Parkyns told him that he was privileged because he'd never tried that move on anyone before.

The wrestling baronet's tomb can still be seen in Bunny Church, with an image of Sir Thomas wearing his wrestling gear.

FOUR

WORKING CHILDREN

EDWARD PEPPER

Edward Pepper is my name, but you can call me Eddie,
I wake in the morning to the factory bell,
I spend all day working in hell,
What it's like I really cannot tell,
But I'd rather be a beggar on the street.

Edward Pepper is my name, but you can call me Eddie,
I'm nearly thirteen years of age
But I feel like a tiger locked up in a cage,
My heart is pounding and bursting with rage,
I'd rather be an orphan on the street.

Edward Pepper is my name, but you can call me Eddie,
At night I dream of being free,
Of equality, fraternity and liberty,
But I don't see how that can ever be
I'll still be a orphan on the street.

> Edward Pepper is my name, but you can call me Eddie,
> I don't think childhood should be this way
> There'll come a time when there's no work just play,
> But it won't be in mine or my children's day
> We'll still be workers on the street.

Some years ago I was invited to do some work with the children from Cuckney Primary School, near Worksop. They had been doing research into the history of their very unusual school and wanted to present it in the form of a song. Together we wrote one about Edward Pepper, a real child who had lived about 200 years earlier. The pupils wrote about eight verses and a tune. It was very good, so good in fact that I took the tune, cut the words down to four verses and polished it up to sing myself. It's on my CD, *The Jenny & the Frame & the Mule*. So who was Edward Pepper, and why is Cuckney Primary School special?

Most schools are housed in buildings designed for that purpose. Over the years they have changed; Victorian schools are often large, forbidding buildings with high windows to stop the children from seeing out. Modern schools are more likely to be single story, light and airy. Cuckney school is neither because it was not designed as a school but as a cotton mill. The mill, and indeed the village, was owned by the Duke of Portland who lived at nearby Welbeck Abbey. The mill obviously did not prove very successful because it ceased production in 1844, and two years later the Duke had it converted into a National School for Boys and Girls. But it still looks like a mill, perched on the edge of the river.

And Edward Pepper? Well, in the early years of the nine-teenth century he was just one of hundreds of poor orphans on the streets of Tottenham in London. This is his story.

Edward Pepper was about eight years old and managed to keep himself alive by begging, finding the odd coin in the gutter and perhaps even stealing. As well as trying to keep the flesh on his own bones he also had a younger brother to care for, no easy task.

And then, one day, he had a stroke of luck, or so it seemed at the time. He met a man who promised him a far easier life. Fair enough, it was far away in a place called Nottinghamshire, which he'd never heard of, but it was in the countryside; there would be fresh air, food would be provided, he would have clothes and a place to live . . . and all he had to do in return was a bit of light work.

So, along with a host of other orphans and street chil-dren of both sexes, Edward went off to Cuckney in north Nottinghamshire to start life as a factory hand in Cuckney Mill.

It was nothing like he had been told. From the start he found himself locked up in what amounted to a prison. He worked from dawn 'til dusk amidst the din and danger of machinery, and rarely even glimpsed the outside world. He'd been promised wages but he didn't see them because anything he earned was taken off him to pay for his food and clothing. Pretty soon Edward realised that, if life as a beggar in London had been hard, it was not as hard as life as a factory child in Nottinghamshire.

What was he to do? Edward Pepper resolved to run away. One summer Sunday afternoon, one of the few times when the children weren't working flat out, he found the opportunity to slip off without being noticed. He ran until he could run no longer and then walked until he was exhausted. By then he was far away from Cuckney so he slept under a hedge. Over the next week or so, Edward Pepper made his way back to London. Sometimes he managed to get a lift on a carrier's wagon but usually he was too scared of being caught and sent back so he walked most of the 200 miles.

At last he found himself in the familiar streets of Tottenham. He was home! He settled back into his old ways, but he soon met people in authority who knew him and they asked him what he was doing back in London. 'Why aren't you working in the factory?' they asked.

He had to think of a reason quickly. He came up with an answer that satisfied them, at least for a little while. 'The factory burned down,' he said, 'so I had to come home.' And then the people thought, 'If the factory has burned down and Edward has come home, where are all the other children?' So they made enquiries.

Edward Pepper was taken back to Cuckney and back to work. He worked there until he became a teenager and then he was 'set free' or, in other words, he was sacked because when he reached the age of fourteen he would have had to be paid a man's wage. It was cheaper to import orphans and sack them when they reached adulthood.

What happened to Edward Pepper after that we don't know; but I guess he probably returned to Tottenham again, and this time stayed there for good.

Nottinghamshire is not famous for cotton mills, unlike neighbouring Derbyshire. This is probably down to the geography. In the early years of the Industrial Revolution mills needed deep valleys with fast-flowing streams which could be easily dammed and used to drive waterwheels. Derbyshire is more suited to that as much of Nottinghamshire is quite flat, or at most gently rolling. There were a few other mills besides Cuckney though, and similar stories to Edward's.

ROBERT BLINCOE

Gonalston Mill was on the Dover Beck, just outside Lowdham. It had been built years before as a corn mill, but with the rise of the cotton industry and the fortunes made by people like Richard Arkwright and Jedediah Strutt it was converted by the owner, Alice Needham, to spin cotton. As at Cuckney, the mill was worked by orphans, this time from St Pancras. One of them was called Robert Blincoe. Robert was just seven years old when, in 1799, he was persuaded to leave the workhouse in London and sign on as an apprentice factory hand after being promised that he and his friends 'would be fed on roast beef and plum pudding, be allowed to ride on their masters' horses and have silver watches and money in their pockets.'

So bad were conditions at the mill that news of the children's mistreatment led to the St Pancras authorities – who had sent them to Gonalston in the first place – setting up a committee of enquiry. Gonalston was closed down and the children moved to Litton Mill in Derbyshire. Talk about 'out of the frying pan into the fire', for Litton was one of the most notorious of all the mills using child labour.

Gonalston Mill still exists. For many years it was derelict but it has now been converted into a private house. Robert Blincoe's story is known because, in 1832, he published a pamphlet called 'Memoir of Robert Blincoe: an orphan boy, sent from the workhouse of St Pancras, London, at seven years of age to endure the horrors of a cotton mill, through his infancy and youth, with a minute detail of sufferings'.

FIVE

FAIRY TALES

Now we move on to something entirely different. Let's leave real-life Nottinghamshire characters, and consider folk-lore and fairy tales, tales which might well have appealed to Edward Pepper and Robert Blincoe if there had been anyone around to tell them to them.

This little group of stories were all collected by Sydney Oldall Addy in the last quarter of the nineteenth century. Addy lived in what was then the village of Norton in Derbyshire – it's now a suburb of Sheffield. By profession he was a solicitor but his hobby was collecting old songs and stories, rhymes, traditions, dialect words and anything else he found interesting. He also excavated prehistoric sites, studied buildings and wrote for all kinds of magazines and learned journals.

At the time of his death in 1933, Addy's most important work was considered to be on vernacular buildings, particularly the history of the English house, but he is best known amongst folklorists and storytellers for his book *Household Tales & Traditional Remains Collected in the Counties of York, Lincoln, Derby & Nottingham*, which he published in 1895. Since then most other tellings of these stories have been based on his versions.

Addy collected most of his stories in Derbyshire and around Sheffield, and with these he noted both the place they were collected and a bit of information about the informant who gave them to him. He collected far fewer stories in Nottinghamshire and did not say where he found them, other than simply stating 'Nottinghamshire'. Many of them are very short, even fragmentary. Here is a selection.

THE LITTLE WATERCRESS GIRL

This is a very strange story which teaches an odd sort of morality. Addy collected a very similar tale in Derbyshire but there, instead of selling watercress, the little girl sold oranges.

There was once a little girl who made her living by selling watercress. Sometimes she would stand on the street corner and cry her wares: 'Water-creases, fresh water-creases.'

At other times she would go round from house to house in the town and knock on doors to see if the housewife wanted to buy any watercress. One day she met an old witch who said to her, 'If you will come and keep house for me I will sell all your watercress for you.'

The little girl said she'd be very pleased to and promised to work hard, for she thought it would be better keeping house than standing outside in the wind and weather. When they reached the old witch's house the witch said, 'If I am going to help you there is one thing you must promise me, you must never look up the chimney!'

The girl promised that she would never look up the chimney and she went to live at the witch's house and helped her with the housework. Every day as she was working around the house she kept thinking about the chimney. I'm sure that if the witch had not said anything about not looking up the chimney the little girl would never have thought of doing so, but now the idea grew and grew in her mind. 'Why must I not look up the chimney?' she wondered. 'I'm sure it wouldn't matter if I just had one little peep.'

She managed to resist the temptation for a few more days but, in the end, it grew too much and she knelt down and peeped up the chimney. At first she could see nothing, just darkness and soot, but then she saw a glimmer of whiteness; there was something wedged up there. She reached up and pulled it down. It was a bag. When she opened it she found that it was full of money. She had never seen so much money before and, although she knew it was wrong, she decided to keep it for herself.

The little girl took the bag of money out into the orchard where many different fruit trees grew. First she went up to the apple-tree, and said:

> Apple-tree, apple-tree, please hide me,
> And if anyone should ask you if you've seen me
> Please say 'I have not.'

The apple-tree promised to hide her.

When the witch came back and found that her bag of money was gone she looked everywhere for the little water-cress girl. She searched all through the house, and then she went into the orchard.

First of all she went to the gooseberry bush, and said:

>Gooseberry-bush, gooseberry-bush
>Have seen a little girl with a white bag in her hand?
>The gooseberry-bush said, 'I have not.'

Then the witch went to the pear tree and said:

>Pear-tree, pear-tree
>Have seen a little girl with a white bag in her hand?
>The pear tree said, 'I have not.'

Then the witch went to the plum tree and said:

Plum-tree, plum-tree

Have seen a little girl with a white bag in her hand?

The plum tree said, 'I have not.'

The witch went to every tree in the garden and asked them all the same question, but all the trees replied, 'I have not.'

At last the witch came to the apple tree and said:

Apple-tree, apple-tree

Have you seen a little girl with a white bag in her hand?

And, like all the other trees, the apple tree said, 'I have not.'

So the witch went home to bed, and when she had gone the little girl carried the bag of money home and didn't go back to the witch's house ever again.

JACK AND THE BUTTERMILK

Apart from Robin Hood and the stories of the 'Wise Men of Gotham', Jack and the Buttermilk is probably the most widely anthologised of all Nottinghamshire stories. Buttermilk is the liquid left after butter has been made from cream.

Jack was a boy who sold buttermilk. One day, as he was going on his rounds from house to house, and hamlet to hamlet, he met a witch. She asked him for some of his buttermilk and told him that if he refused to give it to her, she would put him into the bag she carried over her shoulder and take him to her house, where she'd cook him and eat him for her dinner.

Jack didn't want to give the witch any of his buttermilk because he and his family needed every penny he could earn from selling it so he refused, and the witch grabbed him and put him into her bag and started off home. But, as she was going along the way, she suddenly remembered something: she'd bought a large pot of oil in town but had left it in the shop to collect later. The bag, with Jack in it, was too heavy to carry all the way back to town, so the witch asked some men who were cutting the hedge by the roadside if they would look after it until she came back. The men promised to take care of the bag and the witch hurried off back to the town.

When the witch had gone Jack started to shout. 'Hello!' he called. 'Please will you take me out of this bag and fill it full of thorns, and if you do I will give you each some of my buttermilk.' So the men took Jack out of the bag and filled it with thorns which they had cut from the hedge. Then Jack gave them each some buttermilk and ran home as fast as he could.

When the witch came back from the town she picked up her bag, threw it over her shoulder, and set off home. She'd not gone far before the thorns began to prick her back and she said, 'Jack, Jack, I think you've got some pins in that sack with you, my lad.'

As soon as she got home she tipped up the bag onto a clean white sheet that she had ready. She was expecting a boy to tumble out but, instead, there was just a pile of thorns. The witch was very angry and said, 'I'll catch you tomorrow Jack. And then I'll boil you up for my dinner!'

The next day she met Jack again and once again she asked him for some buttermilk and told him that if he refused to give it to her she would put him into her bag and carry him home and cook him up for dinner. Again Jack refused to give her any buttermilk so she grabbed him and put him into her bag and set off home. But again she remembered that she had left something behind in town so she would have to go back to fetch it. This time she left the bag with some men who were breaking up stones to mend the road. Now, as soon as the witch had gone Jack called out to them and said, 'Please will you take me out of this bag and fill it full of stones, and if you do I will give you each some of my buttermilk.' So the men took Jack out of the bag and filled it with some of the stones which they were using to mend the road. Then Jack gave them each some buttermilk and ran home as fast as he could.

When the witch came back from the town she picked up her bag, threw it over her shoulder, and set off home. As she was trotting along she heard the stones grinding and rattling and she chuckled to herself and said, 'My word Jack, your bones do crack.' When she got home she emptied the bag onto the white sheet again. When she saw the stones she was very angry and said, 'I'll catch you tomorrow Jack. And I'll boil you, I swear it!'

The next day she went out as before and met Jack again. She asked him for some buttermilk and again Jack refused to give her any so, without more ado, the witch grabbed Jack and stuffed him into the bag and ran straight home with him, not giving him any chance to escape from the bag.

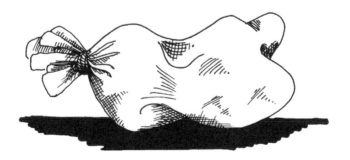

When she reached her house she left Jack tied up in the bag and went out, locking the door securely behind her. She was going to boil him when she returned. While she was away Jack wriggled and scrambled and pulled and tugged and managed to get himself out of the bag. Then he opened all the cupboards in the house and filled the bag with all of the witch's best china. Then he left the bag lying where the witch had left it and climbed up the chimney and escaped.

When the witch came back she picked up the bag and roughly emptied it onto the sheet again. She did it so roughly that she hadn't an unbroken piece of china left in the house. She was very angry and swore that she would catch Jack and teach him a lesson. Next time she would boil him up and eat him straight away, before he had a chance to escape. But she never managed to catch Jack ever again so she was never able to do it.

What is it about witches and buttermilk? The following tale is of yet another witch trying to get buttermilk without paying for it.

THE WITCH AND THE BUTTERMILK

In a certain village in Nottinghamshire there lived a farmer and his wife. One day, their son got married and brought a beautiful young wife home to his parent's house. As well as getting to know her husband and his parents she had to learn the ways of the village and about the people who lived there.

In that same village there lived an old woman who was said to be a witch. The farmer and his wife used to give her buttermilk whenever she came and asked for it. One day, the young wife happened to be in the dairy when the old woman came and asked for her buttermilk. The girl said, 'I'm sorry but we've no buttermilk to spare today.' So the old woman went away without any.

Soon afterwards the young wife started to make butter. She put the buttermilk into the churn and started to turn the handle but, try as she might, the butter wouldn't come, and she wondered why – she was doing everything as she had been taught and she had done it hundreds of times before. But making butter is a tricky, almost magical, process. Sometimes the butter comes easily in no time at all, and at other times you can churn and churn and it just won't happen. After a while her husband called to say that dinner was ready so she left the butter making, intending to start again when she'd eaten.

Whilst they were eating their dinner the farmer said, 'I wonder why old Sarah hasn't fetched her buttermilk today.'

'Well,' said the young wife, 'an old woman did come by this morning asking for buttermilk, but I told her we had none to spare.'

'Then you can put your churn away,' said the farmer, 'and forget all about making butter this week because old Sarah won't let it come. You didn't know but you must always give old Sarah buttermilk when she wants it or she will bewitch the cream.'

THE WEAVER'S WIFE AND THE WITCH

There was a weaver and his wife who lived at Sutton-on-Trent. One day, the weaver set off to Newark to sell his linen, as he often did. His wife was ill so he left her in bed and he told his children to look after her while he was gone.

Now, nearby there lived a witch who had a grudge against the weaver's wife. She wanted to do some spiteful deed against her; why, I don't know, that's probably another story.

A short time after the weaver had gone, one of the children, a little girl, heard a noise; it sounded as if something was pattering up and down the stairs. The girl opened the door at the bottom of the stairs and there, in front of her, was a great, ugly cat. She tried to catch it but it kept springing out of the way or slipping between her legs. However much she tried, she could not get hold of it.

Then the cat bounded up the stairs, leaped onto the sick woman's bed and clawed her face. The woman knocked the cat onto the floor, it hissed and disappeared out of the door.

That night, when the weaver came back from Newark, the children told him about the cat. He suspected that it wasn't an ordinary cat so he sat up to keep watch. He saw the cat come in and leave again through a broken windowpane in the lumber room, but he still couldn't catch it.

A few nights later the cat came in as the weaver was sitting by the fire, so he picked up the toasting fork and stabbed at it. He struck it on the cheek. Then he picked it up and threw it

out of the door, believing that it was dead. In the morning he went to look for the cat's body but he couldn't find it.

For ever after that the witch had her face tied up in a hand-kerchief and she could cast no more spells and do no more harm to the weaver or his family.

THE WITCH AND THE PLOUGHMAN

There was once a rich farmer who kept many servants, all who worked in his house and on his farm. Near to his house lived a witch and the farmer often told his servants that if she asked them to give her anything they should do so at once; they should never refuse her. One day, the farmer hired a new ploughman and said to him, 'If the old witch from up the road asks you for anything you must give it to her straight away, with no argument.'

'I shall give the old lass nothing!' the ploughman muttered to himself.

One day soon after that he met the witch as he was going to work and she asked him to give her something to eat, but he refused. When he reached the field he was going to plough his horses wouldn't go, they just stood in the field. They weren't frightened, they weren't tired, but they were not going to pull the plough. The ploughman saw the witch standing by the hedge so he spoke to her and persuaded her to let them go.

This old witch lived by herself in a lonely little hut in the woods. One day, the ploughman decided he would go and see her, thinking he might give her a fright to teach her not to mess with him in future. He rode up to her hut and knocked at the door. 'Mother, I've come to take you for a ride,' he said.

'Wait till I have suckled my cubs and buckled my shoes and then I will be with you,' said the witch. So she suckled her cubs and buckled her shoes and followed him out. But as soon as the ploughman had mounted the horse she turned herself into a hare and sprang with her claws upon the horse's back. The terrified horse jumped many feet into the air but the ploughman knocked the hare down and killed it on the spot. The farmer and his workers were not bothered by bewitched horses any more.

THE BEWITCHED HORSES

One day, as a carter was leading his horses along the high road, an old woman came up to him and asked him for a pipe of tobacco. The carter said, 'Nay, you must buy your own tobacco, like me.' So the old woman went on her way. The horses had not gone many yards further before they stopped and stood quite still, not moving another inch.

The carter climbed down from his wagon and lay down on the grass by the roadside to think about what he was to do next. As he lay thinking, a stranger came by and said, 'What's the matter; why are you laying there?'

The carter said, 'My horses are bewitched. An hour ago an old woman passed me on the road and asked me for a pipe of tobacco and I wouldn't give it to her. Now she's bewitched my horses.'

The stranger said, 'You ought to have given her what she asked for. You were very foolish to refuse, but do as I tell you and we'll make it alright. Go to the old woman's cottage and get something of hers; either beg, borrow, or

steal it. Then, when she comes near you, scratch her arm with a needle and draw blood.'

So the carter set out to do what the stranger told him. First he called at a house on the road and borrowed a stocking-needle. Then he went to the witch's cottage and said to her, 'I've come to buy a penn'orth o' thread, mother.' The old witch fetched him some thread and, as she was giving it to him, he took the stocking-needle and scratched her arm from elbow to wrist. When he had done this he paid for the thread and took the stocking-needle back to the woman who had lent it to him. Then he ran back to his horses and found that they had started at the very moment he had drawn blood from the witch's arm.

Sometimes magic can be used for good not evil. The following tale is an example, although I'd be very wary of the old man and avoid him if I possibly could.

THE WIZARD OF LINCOLN

There was a farm, just over the county boundary into Lincolnshire, and at that farm there was once a great robbery. They took money, candlesticks, silver plate and cutlery; everything of any worth. Nobody could find the loot and they could not find who the thief was, even though they tried and tried. At last, the farmer's wife had an idea and said to her husband, 'If you will send for the Wizard of Lincoln, he'll tell you.'

The Wizard of Lincoln was not a man with a tall hat and a robe with stars and moons all over it, he looked and dressed like an ordinary man, but he had the reputation of being very wise and knowing everything that was going on. He could solve people's problems and sometimes strange things would happen whilst he was around.

The farmer sent for the Wizard and a few days later he arrived – not as a man but in the form of a large black bird. Now, witches often take the form of hares but wizards seem to prefer birds – usually crows. The bird flew around the farmyard and frightened the cattle so badly that they tried to rush into the barn where a man was threshing wheat.

Then the black bird sat on a post and spoke to the farmer. 'Shall I bring the thieves into your house or shall I just make their shadows appear on the wall?'

The farmer said, 'You do whatever you think is best.'

He had hardly spoken when one of the farm workers who was actually away working in a distant field, seemed to walk through the room.

'That is one of the thieves,' said the bird.

Then he pointed to a shadow on the wall, and the farmer recognised it as the shadow of another of his servants. It was unmistakeable.

'That is the other thief,' said the black bird, and flew away.

The farmer sent for the constable and the two men were arrested. The money and all the other things that they had stolen were found in their room.

THE GOOD MAGPIE

There is a black bird in this story too – perhaps it is a witch or wizard in disguise:

One for sorrow, two for mirth,
Three for a wedding, four for a birth,
Five for a parson, six for a clerk,
Seven for an old man buried in the dark.
(Nottinghamshire version of the well known rhyme)

There was once a gentleman who liked to ride out on his horse every day. One day, he stopped at a house by the road-

side where a woman and her little boy lived. He had business with the woman so he went in to talk to her and he found her in the kitchen heating up the oven. The little boy said to him, 'Mother's holing the oven ready to put me in.' (Holing is a Nottinghamshire way of saying heating up.) The gentleman thought that the boy was only joking so he took no notice, finished his business with the woman, and rode away.

The gentleman had not gone far when a magpie flew across the track in front of him. It kept flying in front of his horse and would not go away. It landed on branches over his head and chattered and squawked and frightened the horse. At last the man decided that the magpie was trying to tell him something; it seemed to want him to turn back. So, he wheeled his horse round and galloped straight back to the house where the woman and the little boy had been. When he got there he found that the woman had gone and the poor little boy was roasting in the oven. He threw open the oven door and pulled the little boy out just in time before any harm could come to him.

THE GOOD FAIRY AND THE BAD FAIRY

Sydney Oldall Addy called the next story 'The Clean Fairy and the Dirty Fairy' but, to me, those names do not seem to describe the fairies properly – perhaps clean and dirty had different connotations in his time. I have changed them to Good and Bad, which would make much more sense to modern children. Many old fairy tales include needless, unexplained, cruelty. Perhaps it is because the stories are only fragments of longer stories in which the events would make more sense, or maybe it is because they were intended as warnings. You can imagine Mama or Papa (or more likely a governess) telling the story and then saying: 'If you are a naughty little girl the Bad Fairy will take you away too!' Addy's story was unfinished so I created the ending.

One day, a bad fairy stole a little girl and took her away to her home inside a fairy hill far away. When the little girl had been there for some time, the bad fairy said she had to go out for a while but she would leave the little girl a task to do, to keep her out of mischief whilst she was gone. She said, 'If you don't finish the task before I'm back you will be in trouble.'

When the girl first saw the task she had to complete she was horrified; there was no way she could get it done in time. The bad fairy had left a huge pile of pins which the girl was supposed to thread in a line on a long strip of paper, for that was the way pins were sold in those days.

The little girl began to cry because she saw that she could not possibly put the pins straight before the bad fairy came back. A good fairy happened to pass by the house in the fairy hill and heard the little girl crying. She came into the house with her wand in her hand, and asked the little girl, 'Why are you crying?'

'I have to put all these pins straight in the paper before the fairy comes back, and I can't do it.'

'Don't worry,' said the good fairy, 'I can do that for you, easily.'

The good fairy waved her wand over the pins and they lined themselves up and stuck themselves through the paper in no time at all.

When the bad fairy came back and found the pins straight in the paper she was amazed, and rather angry. 'I don't know how you did that,' she said, 'but tomorrow I'll set you another task that you definitely won't get done.'

The next day, she went out again and left the little girl with twice the amount of needles as she had given her pins to put straight on the paper. This was even more difficult because needles don't have a nice round head you can use to push them in with, even the end with the eye is sharp and it hurts your finger when you thread the needle through the paper. When the bad fairy had gone the little girl cried and the good fairy came as before and, in no time at all, put the needles straight in the paper by waving her wand.

When the bad fairy came back she said to the little girl, 'Show me the needles,' and she saw that they were all lined up and threaded through the paper. 'I'll set you a job that I know you can't get done,' she said.

So, the next day, the bad fairy brought a great bag full of beads – all different kinds in all different sizes and colours, and told the little girl to thread them in a certain pattern that was very complicated and hard to do. When she had gone the good fairy came again and threaded all the beads by waving her wand across them as she had done before. But this time she did not leave the little girl alone, she waited until the bad fairy came home. When she did, the good fairy scolded her for treating the little girl so badly. She set the bad fairy a task which she could definitely not finish; she had to sweep up every speck of dust in the house and throw it out of the door,

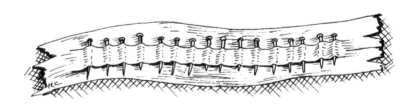

but every time she did so, the wind blew it straight back in and she was kept too busy to work any more mischief.

Pins always used to be sold woven into paper in a row. The motif occurs in the well known folk song:

> I'll give to you a paper of pins
> That's the way our love begins
> If you'll marry me, me, me
> If you'll marry me.

> I'll not accept your paper of pins
> That's not the way our love begins
> I won't marry you, you, you
> I won't marry you.

After many verses, in which he offers many gifts, he eventually finds the thing she wants – usually the key to his heart, and in the end they do marry. That brings us nicely on to stories of love and lovers, probably the most common theme in folklore.

SIX

LOVE STORIES

LOVERS REUNITED

Sir Nicholas was the son of a great lord. He had a sweetheart, Maud, who loved him as much as he loved her, but they knew they would never be allowed to marry while Nicholas's father was alive, for he did not approve of the match; he thought Maud and her family were not suitable. Therefore, Nicholas decided to go away and join the crusade to the Holy Land. He would join the Christian armies fighting to keep Saladin and the Muslims from taking Jerusalem. It would serve to pass the time until his father died; he might earn his fame and fortune as well. He would definitely see the world, have adventures and grow to be a mature man.

Sir Nicholas made his farewells to his love. He swore that he would return and that, one day, they would be married. Before he left they broke a ring in two; Maud kept one half in a purse on her belt and Nicholas took the other with him. It was an idea which they had heard about from old ballads and they thought it was a very romantic thing to do.

Nicholas had all kinds of adventures in Jerusalem. He fought well and gained a reputation as a soldier. He killed many of the enemy and was wounded himself but, eventually, he was captured by the Saracens and locked up in a prison cell where he was kept for seven years, where he suffered from beatings, ill-treatment and near starvation. The only thing that kept Sir Nicholas sane were his memories of Maud, who he knew would be waiting for him at home. Towards the end of that time he caught a fever and was near to death. In his ravings Sir Nicholas spoke of Maud and of his home and wished, above all else, that he could fall asleep and wake up in the church porch of his beloved home town, Sutton in Nottinghamshire.

And he did.

I don't know how he got there and Sir Nicholas never found out either. You can make up all kinds of possible scenarios as to how it happened and we'll never know which, if any, is correct. Who rescued him from the prison? Was he set free or did he escape? Did the gaoler hear his ravings and feel sorry for him? Was it the gaoler's daughter who fell in love with him, as in the ballad of Lord Bateman? How did he make the long and arduous journey from Jerusalem to England? Did he travel alone or was he carried by friends? Did he come overland or was he put on board a ship? All Sir Nicholas knew was that, after what seemed to be years of jumbled, disconnected, nightmarish images, the fever had suddenly abated his mind became clear, and he opened his eyes and saw the place he most wished to see. At first he could not believe it. He thought it was yet another hallucination. But then he realised that he was at home in Sutton. The church and the views were real, not just yet another dream.

Sir Nicholas immediately made his way to the hall where Maud's family lived and asked after her. Unrecognised, he was told that she was preparing to distribute the dole, the

charity which she had instigated in memory of her beloved who had died whilst on a crusade to the Holy Land. He was told that she had done this on this day for the past seven years. Sir Nicholas demanded to be taken to her but no one would take any notice of a sick, ragged, bearded traveller who looked as though he hadn't a penny in the world. But, Sir Nicholas was not going to be denied. He forced his way past the servants and into Maud's chamber. She did not know him and recoiled in fright until he produced his half of the ring.

The two halves were reunited, as were Sir Nicholas and the Lady Maud. His father had died whilst he was away and Sir Nicholas inherited the family's lands and houses and they put their lives back together.

THE LEGEND OF ST CATHERINE'S WELL

Lady Isabel de Caudwell lived in Newark. She was a rich and noble lady and was in the enviable situation of being wooed by two equally eligible suitors – Sir Everard Bevercotes and Sir Guy Saucimere. Both of these worthy knights loved the lady dearly and each tried to outdo the other in competing for her hand. They showered her with gifts and did chivalrous deeds, trying to surpass the achievements of the other and gain the advantage in their competition for the lady's hand.

At last, after many months of courting, Lady Isabel made her decision. She chose Sir Everard and invited him to visit her, secretly, late that evening; the evening of St Catherine's Eve.

When Sir Guy discovered their deceit he was so angry he vowed he would take revenge on both his rival and the woman

who had spurned him. He went to Lady Isabel's house and lay in wait nearby. He watched Sir Everard arrive and followed him into the garden where he was greeted by Lady Isabel. He saw them embrace and, overcome with jealousy, Sir Guy drew his sword and rushed at them. Before Sir Everard had a chance to protect himself he was dead. A fountain of pure water gushed out of the ground on the spot where he fell.

Lady Isabel de Caudwell was inconsolable. She clung to the body and had to be forcibly taken indoors. For days and weeks she was unable to recover from the dreadful event. Eventually she left Newark and a short while later died of a broken heart.

At first, Sir Guy Saucimere was so eaten up with anger that he didn't know or care what he had done, but when time calmed him and the truth of his deed sunk in he was overcome with guilt and despair. He too left Newark and travelled to Nottingham. The change of town didn't help. He could not forget what he had done. He left Nottingham and travelled around the country looking for novelties and entertainments to fill his mind and make him forget the past. But that didn't work either. Finally, he went abroad and travelled the pilgrim roads throughout Europe and the Holy Land. Somewhere on his journey he became infected with leprosy and was covered in sores. This, he thought, was 'God's Righteous Judgement' for his sins.

At last Sir Guy hid himself away deep in the forest of St Avoid in France. Then, one night, he had a strange dream. In the dream, St Catherine appeared to him and told him to return home because the only cure for his sores was the water from the spring where his rival had died.

Sir Guy returned to Newark and bathed in the spring; when he emerged his skin was as pure as that of a newborn baby. From that point on he devoted all his life to God. He built a chapel dedicated to St Catherine near to the spring, which he paved and enclosed with a wall. He also built a basin for the spring to flow into to make it easier for bathers. He became known as St Guthred by the local people and lived for many years as a good and pious man.

St Catherine's Well became famous for its cures and was a popular place of pilgrimage for centuries. It still exists and is still visited, although it is now in the garden of a private house and anyone wanting to take the cure has to get permission from the owners.

St Catherine's Eve is 24 November. St Catherine, of Catherine Wheel fame, is the patron saint of those who work with cloth and needles: sewers and embroiderers; lace makers and the like. She is also the saint to whom women turn to for help with all kinds of feminine ailments. In France they call the menopause 'turning St Catherine's corner'.

LOVE ACROSS THE DIVIDE

This is one of the stories retold by John Potter Briscoe in *Nottinghamshire Facts and Fictions*. He called it 'The Maid of Broxtowe and the Republican Officer' and described it as 'a Broxtowe tradition'. It takes place a couple of hundred years after the previous two tales and is a love story which takes place against the backdrop of the English Civil War.

The year is 1645. The two main characters are Agnes Willoughby and Captain Thornalgh, who both came from good families. She was a beautiful young woman and he was a handsome young man. In many ways they were an ideal match. But I have called the tale 'Love Across the Divide', for the divide was huge. Agnes Willoughby was the daughter of the owner of Aspley Hall; her family was Catholic and Royalist. Captain Thornalgh, on the other hand, was a Republican and a Puritan; the commander of the garrison at Broxtowe Fort on the outskirts of Nottingham. Normally, in those times, the two would never have had anything to do with each other. The way in which they met though, almost guaranteed that they would fall in love.

One day, Agnes was walking alone. She had been to visit a poor sick man in the nearby village of Bilborough and was making her way home when she was set upon by a gang of young men. The countryside was full of such young men at that time; not quite soldiers, not quite outlaws, but flitting between the two occupations depending on which way of life was to their best advantage at that particular moment. The three men had followed Agnes for a while and they leapt out at her when she entered a dark wood. She was on the ground and fighting for her life, or at least her honour; she did not mind if she only lost her money. She had no hope of being heard if she screamed.

Captain Thornalgh happened to be out walking too. He was wandering far from his fort, deep in thought, when he heard a woman's cry. He ran towards it and found Agnes on the ground, kicking and screaming and trying to fight off the three men. Thornalgh drew his pistol and fired. He hit one of the men and the others ran off. Thornalgh then helped Agnes to her feet and calmed her and then insisted on walking her home to Aspley Park. He was aware of her family's political and religious persuasions and knew that he would not be welcome there. Agnes knew from his dress what and who Thornalgh was. They both knew that any kind of relationship between them would be impossible, but they both felt an immediate attraction and commonsense often plays second fiddle when the theme is love.

Thornalgh delivered Agnes safely into the care of her family, who were grateful to him for saving their daughter. But they were not too welcoming to their enemy. The next day he visited Aspley again and was granted a meeting with Agnes.

By now they were inextricably set on the path towards . . . what? They both wanted marriage; both of their families would consider no such thing. Neither of them was willing to change their religious beliefs. They could not be together but neither could they bear the idea of being apart.

As is so often the case, the impasse was solved by the army. Thornalgh was on his knees praying for an answer to his problems when a messenger arrived from Colonel Hutchinson at Nottingham Castle. Thornhalgh was to bring as many men as could be spared from Broxtowe and go to Nottingham and then on to Newark, with Hutchinson's army, to reinforce the siege of the town which was a Royalist stronghold. He just had time to get a message to Agnes before he was on the road with his men. On the way to Newark the army stopped to attack Shelford Manor, which was also held by the Royalists. The manor was heavily fortified and defended by powerful guns as well as many troops. The battle was hard and Thornalgh led his men bravely, but in an assault on the house he took a musket ball to the heart and died instantly.

Agnes had received the news of the march with a sense of foreboding. She shut herself in her room and devoted her time to praying to the Holy Virgin for guidance. She was not surprised to hear of her true love's death, for she had felt that it was bound to happen.

She immediately put aside all her rich clothes and all the plans which her parents might have made for her future. She dressed herself in rough, black clothing and retired to a simple cottage, where she spent the rest of her long life living simply; fasting, praying and giving alms to the poor. She died much loved and missed by all the people around. She herself though, died happy, with the thought that she could now be reunited with the man she loved.

THE SHOEMAKER OF SOUTHWELL

It was Midsummer's Day in the summer of 1645; 'flaming June', beautiful summer weather in the heart of England. But King Charles I could not enjoy it. A few weeks earlier, at a place called Naseby down in Leicestershire, his army had been utterly destroyed and the King himself had narrowly escaped with his life. Luckily for him, Cromwell's men did not follow him when he fled north; they had more urgent matters to attend to in the south west. He had taken refuge in Southwell whilst he decided what to do next. There was little support left for his cause in the south and he doubted that there was here, in Nottinghamshire, either.

With a small group of his closest friends he took lodgings at the King's Head Inn. He was dressed plainly and kept a low profile so no one, not even the landlord of the inn, knew who he was.

The King was weary and worried. He was tired but he couldn't sleep. He decided to go for a walk. Just opposite the King's Head was the Minster, so he went in and spent some time praying for guidance and for the souls of the men who had been killed in the recent battle. As he sat in the church he looked at his boots and noticed how worn they were. He needed new boots. You can't be a king with holes in your boots. There must be a shoemaker in Southwell, he thought, and he set out to find him.

At length the King found the shoemaker's shop and went in. He told the shoemaker that he was a visitor to the town, staying at the King's Head, but he needed some new boots as quickly as possible. The shoemaker was helpful and assured his customer that he could make him a fine pair of boots and he would do it as quickly as he could without sacrificing quality. The King paid in advance and the shoemaker started to measure the King's feet and to draw round them with chalk on a board.

Now, when a tradesman has his customer in a corner he will start talking. It doesn't matter whether he is a shoemaker, a tailor, a barber or a taxi-driver, he will make sure his customer shares his wisdom and ideas; he will put the

world to rights. While he measured the King's feet, the shoe-maker told him of the strange dream he had had that night; a dream which had puzzled and worried him. He dreamed he had been in London, although it was a place he had never been to and was unlikely ever to go to. There, in the middle of the city in a grand street he had seen a noble gentleman with long curling hair and a beard standing on a dais sur-rounded by a hostile crowd. He didn't know what was going to happen to the gentleman but he could sense that it wasn't good. The shoemaker was frightened and wanted to wake up, but he couldn't. Then, in his dream, he asked another man in the crowd who the lone gentleman was. He was told that the man was doomed and anyone who helped him or sympa-thised with him was doomed too.

The shoemaker was obviously still unnerved by the dream and the King felt sorry for him.

'Then what happened in your dream?' he asked.

'I don't know,' replied the shoemaker, 'for I woke up. And very pleased I was to do so.'

The King rose and walked to the window. He took off his hat so that the light fell on his face and the shoemaker instantly recog-nised the doomed gentleman from his dream. He was now even more scared. 'I'm sorry, sir,' he said, 'but I have to think of my business. I have a wife and family to care for. I cannot risk upset-ting the townsfolk. I am sorry, but I cannot make your boots.'

The King said that it didn't matter, he would not insist. He gave the shoemaker a handful of coins and returned to the inn with his old boots on his feet.

When the shoemaker realised just who the man in his dream was, I don't know, but I assume he must have eventu-ally put two and two together.

THE FAIR MAID OF CLIFTON

Ye gallant dames so finely framed in beauty's choicest mould
And you that trip it up and down like lambs in Cupid's fold
Here is a lesson to be learned of a peculiar kind
By such as do prove false in love and bear a faithless mind.

This tale brings us another 150 or so years nearer to the present. It exists in various forms but the best known is a poem written by the teenaged poet, Henry Kirk White, in 1801. The first verse is written above. It shares many ideas and motifs with the previous stories and I wonder whether they have gradually grown to resemble each other (naturalists would call it 'convergent evolution'), or whether they might all be versions of the same story adapted to suit the times in which they were told?

In the village of Clifton, not far from Nottingham, lived a fair young maiden called Margaret. Margaret came from a wealthy family and her prospects were good which, alone, would have made her very interesting to any local gentleman, but Margaret was also very attractive with rosy cheeks and dark, shiny hair. She had a ready laugh and a flirtatious manner and made every man who had anything to do with her feel that he was her favourite and the only man in the world who really stood a chance of marrying her. Not surprisingly, therefore, gentlemen young, and not so young, from all over Nottinghamshire beat a path to Margaret's door.

Despite all this interest, the wooing and the love making, Margaret remained aloof and refused to finally commit to any one man. She rode out with them individually or in groups; she invited them to garden parties and picnics; she exchanged teasing love letters with them, and accepted their generous gifts; she played them all along like an angler up to his thighs in the Trent plays a fish, keeping them all interested but not saying or doing anything definite.

Until Young Bateman came along that is.

Young Bateman was by no means the richest of her suitors and if his prospects were analysed coldly he would not have been anywhere near the top of the list of suitable husbands for Margaret, but love is a strange thing. Margaret and Young Bateman felt that immediate attraction which is not based on analysis and logic, but on emotion and the heart.

Gradually Margaret stopped seeing the other suitors. If they called she was out; their letters went unanswered; invitations to ride out with them were returned saying that she had a previous engagement. She only had time for Young Bateman. They met sometimes in public, with her parents and other friends; but they met far more often, secretly, in quiet spots around the countryside where they would walk arm-in-arm and talk of their love for each other. Their favourite spot for such trysts was by the river in Clifton Grove. Here the Trent runs between small cliffs and the banks are clothed with ancient woods. It is a quiet place where fish leap and birds sing. In the Grove they could be alone with little fear of meeting anyone else.

Soon Margaret and Bateman exchanged promises that nothing but death itself would ever separate them. They became engaged, although it was kept as their secret for the moment, even kept from their parents. This serene state of affairs continued for three months. Bateman went around in a haze of love with his mind full of Margaret, his head in the clouds and a silly smile on his face. He had never been so happy.

To cement their engagement the couple followed a tradition which they knew of from old songs; they broke a coin
in half and Margaret kept one half and gave the other half
to Bateman. It was a symbol that they were each half of a
whole; neither was complete without the other.

And then Margaret's engagement was announced. Her
engagement to old Germain! Old Germain the rich, grumpy
widower who had nothing to offer Margaret but his fortune
and his early death. Overnight, she denied ever having promised anything to Bateman. She laughed at the very idea of it
and called it wishful thinking. She did, however, admit that
she had walked out with him 'a few times' but said it meant
nothing, he was just a friend of her own age with whom
she could have fun. 'There never was any talk of love and
definitely no arrangement regarding marriage,' she swore.
Bateman produced his half of the coin but Margaret said she
knew nothing about it. It was all in his imagination.

Bateman was heartbroken, hurt and furious. He swore that
either he would have Margaret or that she would never have
a moment's peace for the rest of her life. 'I will make you
sorry for what you have done,' he said. 'I will have you alive
or dead; on earth or in my grave. I will make you suffer as I
am suffering. I will make sure that you never forget me until
the day you die.' He stormed out of her house and wasn't seen
again until the day of her wedding.

When the morning of the wedding of Margaret and
Germain dawned, Margaret was awoken by moans and
cries. She stumbled from her bed and crossed to the window.
When she peered through the curtains a terrible sight met
her eyes. With a cord around his neck Bateman was hanging
from a tree writhing and moaning. His eyes were popping

from his head and foam dripped from his mouth. As she looked, their eyes met and she was overtaken by grief. At that moment she realised what she was doing and that she really did love the young man. But it was too late. His body was cut down but he was dead. The wedding was cancelled.

Bateman's threat (or was it a promise?) came true. From that day on Margaret did not have a moment's peace; wherever she went she saw the body hanging from the tree and could heard the strangled cries and gurgles. She could not eat or sleep and her beauty faded. When it all became too much, Margaret returned to the place in Clifton Grove where she and Young Bateman had walked and talked so many times; walked arm-in-arm and talked of spending their lives together. She threw herself from the highest of the cliffs, which border the river, into the water below and was swept away by the Trent. That hillside has remained arid ever since.

SEVEN

TALES FROM THE DARK SIDE

One of my favourite books is Daniel Defoe's *A Tour Through the Whole Island of Great Britain*, in which he describes most of the country as he saw it in the 1720s. He pays scant attention to Nottinghamshire though. He talks about Nottingham: 'one of the most pleasant and beautiful towns in England'; mentions 'prodigious crops of barley' grown beside the Trent, and passes over most of the rest of the county with a paragraph about Sherwood Forest which, he says, is:

> [...] an addition to Nottingham for the pleasure of hunting, and there are also some fine parks and noble houses in it, as Welbeck, the late Duke of Newcastle's, and Thoresby, the present noble seat of the Pierrepont's . . . but the forest does not add to the fruitfulness of the county, for 'tis now, as it were, given up to waste . . . and if there was such a man as Robin Hood . . . he would hardly find shelter for one week if he was now to have been there.

So, Nottinghamshire was a land of ancient, derelict forest dotted with the estates of the nobility and with few settlements off the main roads. If it was in Europe it would seem

to be an ideal setting for tales of wolves and vampires; evil
Counts; and little girls lost in the depths of the dark wood.
The story of the Gypsy Boy is a good introduction to a set of
stories which take up that theme.

THE GYPSY BOY

A young gypsy boy made his way through the forest. He was a
good looking youth, dressed in ragged clothes with curly black
hair and rosy cheeks. He had a small bag on his back which
contained everything he owned. He was in no hurry as it was a
lovely day and he hadn't a care in the world as he whistled while
he walked. For the past few years this had been his life; he'd travelled whenever and wherever the mood took him. He couldn't
remember half the places he had been to and didn't know the
names of the other half, but he had had some exciting adventures and met some interesting people. Now though, he was
beginning to think it was time to settle down, at least for a while.

At length he came out of the trees and found himself in the village of Sherwood, a fitting name for a place on the edge of the vast
forest. It was just a couple of miles from Nottingham. He thought
it might be a good idea to stop there for the night and find out
what was happening and then go on into the city the next day. He
found an inn and begged a drink and a bite to eat and got talking
to a few of the men who were loafing about outside.

'What's the news?' he asked. In return for him telling them
about things he had seen on his travels (and some tall stories
about things they would have liked him to have seen on his
travels, which pleased them even more) they told him about
the goings on locally.

The main story, the one which made him prick up his ears, was about a grand lady in the city who was in need of a husband. No one seemed to know much about this lady or where she had come from, but they were all sure that she wasn't local. Some claimed that she came from some far distant part of Europe; some even believed that she might be a princess, but they were all in no doubt that she was very wealthy. She was, apparently, a mature woman not a young girl, but very striking-looking. 'She speaks with a strange accent,' said one, although he hadn't actually heard her speak himself.

A good-looking, wealthy, mysterious older woman in need of a husband . . . was this just what he was looking for? To be the husband of a Great Lady? That did not seem too onerous a task, so, the next morning he washed at the village pump and ran his fingers through his hair. He brushed the dust and seeds out of his clothing and set off towards Nottingham.

He breasted a rise and found himself looking down a long hill towards the city. He could see the two hills with the castle on the one to his right and the houses and churches clustered on the other to the left. It seemed to be a busy, prosperous place, with smoke rising from hundreds of chimneys, and he could hear the noise and bustle of everyday life, even from this distance. He walked briskly down the hill and entered through the city gate. Then he started to enquire about the lady and where he could find her. Perhaps he should have asked himself why a rich, beautiful lady who was, perhaps, a princess, was having to advertise for a husband, but he didn't, not even when some men in the market place told him that she'd already had seven husbands and they had all disappeared without trace.

He obtained directions to her house and entered the grounds through ornate gates with towers on either side. He walked past cropped lawns studded with tall, well-cared-for trees; he crossed a formal garden which seemed like nothing less than a life-sized tapestry of herbs and bushes enclosed by clipped box hedges; and then he crunched across a wide drive which led up to the front of the house.

He was impressed by the grandeur of it. He had never lived in a house of any kind – his roof was usually the sky or, in the worst of weather, the inside of a barn or cowshed – and here he was, outside what seemed to him to be an immense palace full of all kinds of strange things he had never seen before, things he could not even imagine the uses of.

His natural instinct was to go round to the back of the house, to the servant's door, but he had come to court the lady so he made himself walk steadily up to the grand front door; to climb the half dozen steps and pull on the bell. As he stood waiting for the door to be opened, he realised that there was very little chance of a lady who lived in such a grand house even seeing him, let alone wanting to marry him. By the time he heard the latch being lifted he was expecting someone to shout at him, wave a club at him, or threaten to set the dogs on him if he didn't go away. He was preparing to run for his life.

But it turned out to be far easier than he could have dreamed. The maid who answered the door asked him straight away if he'd come to marry the lady and when he said he had, if the lady would have him, she immediately showed him in and took him upstairs to a waiting room. He was told to help himself to wine and sweetmeats and to sit and be comfortable until the lady appeared.

After a while the door opened and a tall, grand lady, dressed in the latest fashion, entered the room. He could not believe his eyes. She was more beautiful than the stories had told – not beautiful in a pretty way like the milkmaids he'd often flirted with in the fields, but beautiful in a cold, aloof, mature way which made him almost afraid. He could not judge her age. In some ways she looked quite young but then, seen again from a different angle, she looked older and more experienced than anyone could imagine.

She glanced at him briefly and said, 'Yes, he's the kind of man I will marry,' and immediately sent for the butler to make the arrangements. Before the day was done they were man and wife and he was master of a great house.

After the marriage ceremony and the wedding feast, he and the lady went to bed and pleasured each other in the way that newly-weds will do. It was by no means his first time but she showed him things he had not dreamed of and it was the early hours of the morning before he fell into a deep sleep. A few hours later he awoke and turned to embrace his wife but he was alone in the bed. The room was empty but he wasn't worried; a lady is entitled to get out of bed in the night. He went back to sleep and slept late. When he finally awoke there she was, snuggled by his side. 'Did you sleep well?' she asked. He assured her that he had.

This all seemed quite natural until it gradually dawned on him that every night followed the same pattern: his wife would go to sleep in his arms and she would be by his side in the morning but, at some point in the night, she would disappear and be gone for several hours. Where was she going and why? He decided he had to find out.

The next night he only pretended to go to sleep but, with great difficulty, forced himself to stay awake. In the middle of the night his wife got out of bed and put on a large, dark cloak and slipped out of the room. As soon as she had gone he quickly threw on some clothes and followed after her. She left the house, went through the grounds and down a narrow path which led to the churchyard. She made her way past old moss-covered tombs until she came to the more recent burials and there she fell on her knees and started to scoop away the earth. He could not see what she was doing very well because of the darkness and the gravestones that were in the way but soon she stopped digging and, after a minute, he heard the sound of eating . . . chewing and slobbering and the ripping of meat from bones.

He crept closer and saw her on her knees, tearing like a starving woman at what seemed to be a leg of meat.

In horror he stepped out from the shadows and asked her what she was eating. Hardly ceasing her chewing, and with blood dribbling down her chin, she laughed. 'Corpse, you fool,' she said, 'Corpse!'

He realised that she was feasting on the bodies of her seven previous husbands.

A TALE FROM THE GREAT NORTH ROAD

The Great North Road was, as its name suggests, the main road running from London to the North. The writer Geoffrey Trease, who was born and bred in the city, claims that Nottingham is 'the first town in the north – the Trent being the boundary between South and North England'. Where the North begins is very much a thing for personal opinion. Some people would say Watford Gap. I would place the boundary further up, say Chesterfield or Worksop. In some places the Great North Road follows Ermine Street, the Roman road. For most of history it linked all the small towns and villages through which it ran. If you wanted to travel anywhere, other than via tiny lanes and byways which were often impassable, you made for the Great North Road. At regular intervals along it there would be inns and watering places; places where you could take refuge, seek shelter or change horses. In the days of stagecoaches these became much more formalised and large coaching inns grew up in all the major towns along the route. Most are still there. It was only in modern times, with the rise of motor transport, that we decided we did not want to *link* places but to *avoid* them. Villages first, and then small towns were bypassed. Now the A1, the route which the Great North Road developed into, goes through hardly any settlements at all but sweeps through open countryside and the aim is to traverse the whole route without pausing. (Dick Turpin would go green with envy!)

If you are heading southwards on the A1, soon after it enters Nottinghamshire from the north, the road takes a left turn at a roundabout and heads towards Newark. The A614 continues southward towards Nottingham. This area is known as the Dukeries and was the site of many grand houses and stately homes which have preserved the landscape: Clumber Park; Rufford; the 'official' Sherwood Forest where the Major Oak can be found; nearer to Nottingham there is Newstead Abbey, and so on. In the Industrial Revolution some of these landowners discovered coal on their properties and built pit villages, but they tended to be away from the road. D.H. Lawrence describes the landscape well in several of his novels, especially *Women in Love*.

Major roads are quite often settings for adventures. It would be strange if there were no stories set on the Great North Road. One short story concerns T'owd lad, who is perhaps the devil himself, who drives a coach and four at breakneck speed along the road. The whole thing is surrounded by a fire of burning brimstone and the horses are skeletons. No wonder travellers tried to be home before dark.

Here is my personal Great North Road adventure, which is not quite so dramatic but seemed so at the time.

When I was eighteen and at the end of my first term at college near Wakefield in Yorkshire, I was offered a lift down to London on the back of my room-mate's scooter. I should have realised it was not going to go smoothly because the first thing we had to do was siphon petrol out of someone's car to get us going!

We meandered along at about 30mph and by the time we reached Nottinghamshire it was getting dark. We then discovered that the rear light of the scooter didn't work. But we were students, arty students at that, and, for some reason, we had a torch and red tissue paper in our luggage. We continued south with me holding the torch covered with red tissue in my hand, pointing backwards. We rode all through Nottinghamshire like this. Then, just before we reached Stamford, we were stopped by a police car. Understandably, they would not let us continue but escorted us into Stamford and gave us lodgings in a police cell for the night. It's the kind of thing which could have given rise to stories – did motorists pass a strange, flashing, red light as they drove down the A1 . . . was it a UFO? Or was it, perhaps, the eyes of a spectral hound?

'SWIFT NICK' NEVISON

Did you ever hear tell of that hero,
Bold Nevison it was his name,
And he rode about like a brave hero,
And by that he gained a great fame.

Trad ballad

This might be a story from Nottinghamshire; or it might be a story from Kent, or London, or York. It is definitely a story which moves between Kent and Yorkshire and takes in all the places between via the Great North Road. A slice of the action is also set in Newark, which is my excuse for including it here. It's a story filled with perhaps and either/ors. Nothing is written in stone and every account you read insists that the details are different. You might not have heard of 'Swift Nick' Nevison but you do know all about his most famous deed, the ride from London to York which is usually attributed to Dick Turpin. The fact that it was Nevison not Turpin who achieved that feat is one of the few things we can be sure of . . . perhaps.

John, or William (or even, perhaps, James) Nevison – he was known by all those names – might have been born near Pontefract in West Riding of Yorkshire, and if he wasn't it could have been at Wortley near Sheffield. It must have been in or around the year 1639. His father was either a wool merchant or the steward of Wortley Hall. Either way he was in a stable job and the young Nevison had a comfortable upbringing. Young Nevison was always up to mischief and often in trouble and when he was about thirteen years old the law was after him for something fairly serious, it might have been for stealing from his father but we're not sure. Rather than face the music, he ran away to London, where he worked as a brewer's clerk for a few years before taking a ship to Holland, where he became a soldier with the Grand Old Duke of York.

When the wars were over, Nevison returned to England and nursed his ailing father – he was obviously forgiven for his youthful misbehaviour – and when the old man died he put his soldiering skills to use as a Gentleman of the Road: a highwayman. He quickly gained a reputation as a polite and gallant robber who did no physical harm to his victims. He was also handsome and charming to the ladies, the very model of Hollywood's idea of a highwayman.

Nevison plied his trade as a highwayman for the rest of his life until his death in 1684 except, perhaps, for a few years around 1676-81, when he may have served time as a forced labourer in Tangiers. May have . . . one story says he jumped ship and swam ashore before it left England. Such an escape would be in character. There was also an outrageous escape from Leicester Gaol. He was locked up there for a while but escaped by pretending to die of plague. He feigned the illness with the help of an artist friend and some make-up and when he 'died' he was carried out of the gaol in a coffin.

After the escape, Nevison returned to his main base at the Talbot Inn in Newark, where he and his gang were based and from where they made it unsafe to travel along the Great North Road, anywhere between York and Huntingdon. For a while he was mistaken for his own ghost.

And now we come to the famous deed, the ride from Kent to York. Why Nevison was in Kent I don't know, perhaps things had become too hot for him further north, or perhaps he was just after rich pickings in a new landscape, but he apparently robbed a traveller at Gad's Hill, near Rochester, and, fearing that he had been recognised, decided on an amazing plan to give himself an alibi. He caught a ferry across the Thames and then rode to Chelmsford, where he rested for a while. He then rode on to Cambridge and to Huntingdon, where he joined the Great North Road. Stopping regularly for short breaks to rest his horse he eventually reached York at sunset. He had travelled

200 miles in one day.

Nevison's sensible, carefully-paced ride, which preserved the life of both him and his horse, is in direct contrast to the popular image of Turpin's madcap dash at full gallop, scattering travellers and livestock and shooting his guns. Alison Uttley, writing of her childhood in Derbyshire around 1900, mentioned listening to tales of Dick Turpin, 'He galloped along the roads across our valleys riding Black Bess and leaping toll gates.'

On finally reaching York, Nevison stabled his horse, washed, changed his clothes, and then made his way to the bowling green, where he knew the mayor and other important people would be gathered. He made sure he was noticed and spoke to the mayor as he placed a bet on the outcome of the game.

Nevison had obviously been correct when he feared that he had been recognised because he was soon arrested for the Gad's Hill hold-up, but he was able to call on the Lord Mayor of York to give him an alibi – if he had been placing bets and having a conversation with the mayor in York at 8 p.m. how could he have possibly been in Kent that morning? He was found not guilty, although the story of how he had tricked the system soon spread and Nevison became a hero. Even King Charles admired his deeds and it was he who gave Nevison his nickname 'Swift Nick'. That fame and glamour makes it all the more strange that Dick Turpin, who was just a thug – a murderer, a burglar and a housebreaker more than a 'gentleman of the road' – should eventually be given the credit for the ride from London to York and Nevison should fall into obscurity.

At last Nevison's luck did run out. Throughout his career

he had managed to avoid killing anyone, thus preserving his reputation as a 'gentleman' and making sure that the authorities were not too desperate to catch him. Eventually though, he shot and killed a constable who tried to arrest him. A price was put on his head and he was trapped by bounty hunters whilst drinking at the Magpie (or possibly the Plough) Inn at Sandal, near Wakefield. He was taken to York, tried and found guilty.

'Swift Nick' Nevison was hanged at York Castle on 4 May 1684.

For a story with so many discrepancies and variables that seems far too definite a finale. But, perhaps, it is the only definite thing in the whole tale.

THE STRANDED TRAVELLERS

This is a well known urban myth which is told about very many different places all over the country, and which can be set at many times throughout history. I believe this is the original setting: on the Great North Road where it runs through north Nottinghamshire, back in the days of stagecoaches, probably not long after Swift Nick's day. A few years ago I heard the story updated and broadcast as a radio play. It was very atmospheric and very chilling.

There was a young married couple, the only passengers in a coach travelling between two towns on the Great North Road. As they were going through a thickly wooded area of north Nottingham the coach lost a wheel. That kind of mishap was not unusual and so they weren't too worried. The coach driver immediately set off to find help; he needed two or three strong men to help raise the coach to put the wheel back on. He seemed to be gone for a long time. It got dark and cold and the young woman started to worry. What if the coachman had abandoned them and wasn't coming back? She did not fancy spending the night in the coach.

Her husband decided to wander down the road a little way and see if he could see the coachman returning or find a house where they could shelter or something, anything, it didn't really matter what. He couldn't sit there doing nothing. So off he went, leaving his wife huddling in the corner of the coach. Before he went out of sight round the bend he turned and waved. That was the last she saw of him, or anyone else, for a long time. Where had he gone? Was he alright? Had some mishap befallen him? And why hadn't the coachman returned yet?

By now it was pitch dark. No lights could be seen anywhere. The only sounds were those strange, unexplainable noises which you hear in a wood at night; rustling and shuffling and the occasional crack as a twig breaks; all very quiet sounds which are amplified by your imagination until they fill the night.

The woman sat silently in the corner of the coach wishing that she was somewhere else – anywhere else! She may even have started to doze but she was suddenly jerked out of her sleep when there was a thump and the coach rocked. Someone, or something, had leapt onto the roof. Then there started a rhythmical rocking accompanied by a hammering on the roof of the coach and strange, gibbering noises. She couldn't decide whether they were human or animal. But they were terrifying!

I don't know what would have happened if this situation had remained unchanged, the young woman would probably have gone out of her mind, but she became aware of voices and the sound of people approaching. Through the window she saw lanterns. A crowd of people were arriving. She guessed it must be the coach driver with men to help repair the wheel. She hoped her husband was with them too.

And then a voice called out, 'Madam, when I give you the signal you must very quietly get out of the coach and run towards me. Do not look back, just run to me.'

After a few seconds came the call, 'Come now, as quickly as you can!'

She slipped out of the door and did as she was told, but

before she reached the arms of the waiting crowd she could not resist glancing back.

There on the roof of the coach crouched a man, almost naked, with just a few tattered rags around him and with the remains of chains dangling from his wrists. He was gibbering and dribbling and making insane noises, and all the while he was drumming on the roof of the coach with a large, round object which he held in both hands. When she realised what this object was she collapsed. It was the severed head of her husband!

THE WHITE LADY OF NEWSTEAD ABBEY

There are no ghosts associated with the previous stories, although there could easily have been. Ghost stories are a legitimate aspect of folklore but I don't find them very interesting on the whole, and the majority of them which you find in modern books by 'ghost hunters' or 'spiritualists' are not authentic; they are not old. Most have been invented recently and are very vague: '[. . .]this is an old priory so there were monks here so strange things must have happened and there must be evil spirits and ghosts [. . .]'. A strange kind of logic based on a fiction of its own creating. The White Lady of Newstead Abbey does have some basis in history though.

It is not surprising that Newstead Abbey, because of its history, should have accumulated a stock of ghosts (there are several others besides the White Lady). Newstead Abbey was founded by Henry II. It was for monks of the Order of St Augustine who were very rich and privileged, just the kind of monks Robin Hood would have preyed on. When Henry VIII dissolved the monasteries it was granted to Sir John Byron, the

Lieutenant of Sherwood Forest, who was known as 'Sir John Byron the Little with the Great Beard'. The house was eventually passed down through the generations into the hands of Lord Byron, the poet. When he died it was bought by his childhood friend, Thomas Wildman.

At about the same time a young deaf and dumb woman called Sophie Hyatt came to stay with relatives at a nearby farm. Sophie was very shy and carried a slate with her on which to write but, rather than do that, she would avoid people or hide. When the Wildmans realised that she was a fan of Byron's poetry they gave her permission to walk in the grounds whenever she liked and even to take Byron's dog with her. Because of her reclusive habits and because she always wore light-coloured clothing, people began to think of her as a ghost.

Some years later, Sophie's relative died, leaving her unable to support herself. She left the Wildmans a note explaining the situation and set off to Nottingham to catch the coach to London, to make contact with another relative whom, she hoped, would help her. When the Wildmans read the note they felt sorry for the girl and sent a rider off to catch her. They were going to offer her lodgings in the grounds for the rest of her life.

The rider caught up with Sophie outside the Black Boy pub in the Market Square in Nottingham. There he found a great crowd gathered round the body of Sophie, who was lying dead on the ground. She had been run over by a drayman's cart because she didn't hear his shouted warning.

So, although she wasn't able to spend the rest of her life walking through the grounds of Newstead Abbey her ghost still does, particularly along the White Lady's Walk.

THE HAUNTED CAR

I'm not quite sure when the events in this supposedly true ghost story are supposed to have taken place, but I guess it must have been in the late 1960s or early 1970s. I say that because it was a time when ordinary working people were, for the first time, able to buy themselves cars but it was before all the local pits were closed. I can identify with the couple in the story because I had all kinds of 'adventures', or misadventures, with cars at that time too. It was when we were living in Nottingham and bringing up a family with little money. We would manage to get together about £100 or £120 and find a second-hand (or more likely fifth-hand) car, which we hoped would last a year or eighteen months before it fell to pieces or became un-repairable. For some reason it was usually a Morris 1100. Most of the time, the car did last the expected period, although once or twice it was a dud. But that's nothing compared to the following tale.

There was a young couple who lived in Edwinstowe, a village in the heart of Sherwood Forest. He worked in a local pit and his wife had a part-time job at the village shop.

They'd been saving up and decided they could now afford to buy themselves a little car as a run-about, nothing posh, just a second-hand one. They went through the adverts in the local paper until they found one which they could afford. They went to see it and they thought it must be their lucky day because it looked really good and it ran beautifully. They paid the money and took it home.

Over the next few weeks they developed a routine: if he was on the early shift he'd take the car and drive himself to work; if it was late shift his wife would drop him off at work and then keep the car to use herself and he'd get a lift home with a mate.

The first strange event happened one day when he was driving home from work. It was out of the usual routine for he'd worked overtime, a double shift, and it was early morning when he was coming home. He was tired and looking forward to a bath and a good sleep. He saw a milk float up ahead and glanced in the rearview mirror before he pulled out to overtake it. He froze. There was someone in the back seat. He saw them move as the car swayed. He looked again. It was a bloodstained, gore-covered corpse. He screeched to a halt, leaped from the car, and raced up the road to the milkman. He asked the milkman for help and together they slowly approached the car and peered in through the window. There was nothing there. After a very good look around, in and out of the car, they agreed that he was probably suffering from over-tiredness; it had just been a trick of the light or a reflection that he had seen. He got back in the car, drove home and didn't say anything about it.

The second event happened a few days later. This time his wife had the car and she pulled into a filling station for some petrol. It was one of those new-fangled 'self service' ones and as she went into the garage to pay she glanced back at the car and saw someone in it. 'Someone's stealing my car!' she yelled and ran out across the forecourt. She yanked open the door and there, in the back seat, she too saw a bloodstained, mangled corpse.

She screamed and fainted on the spot and when she recovered she told the garage owner what she had seen. He called the police. They could find nothing but they took her seriously and said they would check up on the car's history. When her husband got home that night she told him all about it and he admitted that he had had a similar experience. Not surprisingly, they became very worried and neither of them drove the car for a few days.

Then they had a visit from the police. It turned out that their car had previously been involved in a fatal accident; a lorry had rear-ended it and the back-seat passenger had been killed. Despite that, the car itself had not been too badly damaged and had been repaired and sold.

They sold it again, too, as quickly as they could. They didn't mind selling it for less than they had paid for it, for who wants a haunted car?

THE BLACK DOG OF CROW LANE

Mr Smalley was driving in his trap along Crow Lane. Crow Lane, a lonesome place with an ominous name. He was waiting for it to happen. It had happened many times before and always in the same place. He wasn't worried any more, in fact he would have been more worried if it hadn't happened! Then, out of the corner of his eye he saw a movement. There it was, padding alongside his trap, a large black dog. It didn't look at him, it didn't take any notice at all, but it kept in time with the trotting pony. And then, after a mile or so, it was gone. Mr Smalley didn't see it go; it just wasn't there any more. He knew that none of the people who lived in the area kept a dog like that and, at first, it had frightened him for he knew old stories about ghostly black dogs, but now he just accepted it as one of the sights you saw along Crow Lane. It was almost part of the landscape.

Fifty years later, another Mr Smalley, the grandson of the first, was driving along Crow Lane on his motorcycle. He had been to a dance in Newark and now he was on his way home to Bathley. There was the black dog again. He had often seen it and often tried to run it over. He tried again but missed. The dog didn't seem to do anything particular to avoid being run over by the motorcycle; somehow it just managed to not be in the right place. He had told his friends about the dog but they laughed and told him he'd had too much to drink, but one day he'd taken his father on the pillion and he had seen the dog too and his mother

had told him that his granddad knew all about it. The black dog never did anyone any harm and no one could come up with any meaning to its appearance, it didn't seem to be an omen or to forecast any event. Perhaps it was a real dog, but it would have been a long-lived one; perhaps it was a ghost; perhaps it was just a shadow or a trick of the moonlight. The only way you are likely to find out is to travel along Crow Lane at night yourself and see if you see it too.

Black dogs, often known as 'Shuck', are very common in parts of eastern England, particularly Norfolk. There are all kinds of theories about them. There are very few reports in Nottinghamshire, but the following one combines black dogs and shying horses which links in with the witch stories elsewhere in this book.

Near the village of Laxton (which is best known for the remains of its medieval open field system) is a lane which runs between Parson's Hill and Brokilow Bridge. About one hundred years ago, a certain farmer used to find that his horses always shied there. There was no obvious reason but he explained it by saying that they were frightened by the Brokilow Boggan. A boggan is usually thought of as a goblin-type figure but this one, he said, was a large, black dog like a wolf hound.

THE BESSIE STONE

Along the course of the Great North Road there are, or were, several famous monuments – the eagle on a pillar commemorating French prisoners of war in Napoleonic times at Norman

Cross, near Peterborough, springs to mind. Crossroads were often important places as well, where suicides were buried or the bodies of criminals were exhibited on gibbets, hence the belief that crossroads are haunted. A more recent aspect of roadside furniture are the 'shrines' of flowers or keepsakes, which spring up to mark the scenes of traffic accidents. Although I have just said 'recent aspect' this is not necessarily the case, the Bessie Stone is a marker of this kind but far older.

It is a small cubic stone, similar to a gravestone, which can be found hidden in the grass beside the A60, about 3 miles south of Mansfield. It is near Portland Training College, which caters for young people with disabilities. The words on it read:

THIS STONE IS ERECTED
TO THE MEMORY OF
ELIZABETH SHEPHARD
OF PAPPLEWICK
WHO WAS MURDERED
WHEN PASSING THIS SPOT
BY CHARLES ROTHERHAM
JULY 7th 1817
AGED 17 YEARS.

Young Bessie Shephard set out from her home in Papplewick one morning to seek work in Mansfield. She was successful and found herself a job. To celebrate she bought herself some new shoes and a yellow umbrella. At about 6 o'clock that evening she was seen walking home, but she never arrived. Next morning, the roads were searched and Bessie's body was found in a ditch along with a blood-covered stake from the fence.

Later that day, a young man, Charles Rotherham, a scissor grinder from Sheffield, was caught leaning over a bridge further down the same road near Loughborough. He seemed oblivious to what he had done and to the punishment that awaited him. He'd been drinking in a local tavern, the Hutt, soon after the murder and had spent the evening in the Three Crowns at Redhill, where he had sung a couple of songs and aroused suspicion by trying to sell Bessie's shoes and umbrella.

Rotherham was unable to give a reason why he had committed the murder. He was hanged in Nottingham on 28 July.

BEWARE THE DEVIL THROWING STONES!

People like to give prehistoric, and even natural features Druidic associations. There is a stone standing alone in a field between Ravenshead and Blidworth called the Druid Stone. There is not much of a story to it other than the name. There is no reason for the belief; it is just a nice idea. People have always had a need to make stories about significant geographical features and if one isn't readily available they make one up. That's part of storytelling.

Another stone which some people like to give Druidic links is the Hemlock Stone. Again, there are many theories about it. Some say it is just a natural piece of extra hard limestone left behind when the rest was eroded away. Others agree with this but think that it has been enhanced by ancient man; carved to give the impression of a head. This time, though, there is also a far more interesting story.

Long, long ago there was a very important monastery on the edge of Nottingham. This was Lenton Priory, (Lenton: Leen town, the town on the river Leen, the river which ran around the base of Castle Rock) the home of many monks who kept an endless stream of prayers going up to God. This really annoyed the Devil. He tried every way he could think of to corrupt the monks. He tempted them with food, treasure, women and anything else he could think of; anything just to stop them praying for a few minutes. But to no avail. He may have managed to get the odd one to 'stray from the path of righteousness' but it made no real difference; still their prayers filled the air.

'Well,' he thought, 'if I can't stop them in one way perhaps I can stop them in another.'

He flew to Derbyshire (where he always felt more at home!) to the hill above Peak Cavern, which is also known as The Devil's Arse. There, he quarried for himself an immense rock of hard sandstone and prepared to throw it at Lenton Priory. 'If they are buried under a few tons of rock that will soon stop their praying,' he thought. He took a deep breath, took aim and let fly. But unfortunately, just at the moment he threw, something happened. I'm not sure whether his foot slipped, or something distracted him, or he sneezed or what, but the result was that he missed. Instead of landing smack on Lenton Priory, the stone flew off at an angle and landed about four miles short of its target, near the village of Bramcote, where it stood upright with one end buried in the ground.

It is still there and you can visit it, carefully tucked behind an iron railing with a board telling you all about it.

On the opposite side of Nottingham there used to be a stone, stood next to the church at Kinoulton, with a similar legend attached to it. The old church on the hill fell into disrepair back in the 1700s and was replaced by a new one in the valley. The stone was supposed to have been thrown by the Lincoln Imp. Two imps were sent by the Devil to do as much mischief as possible. An angel quickly turned one to stone before he could do much harm (you can still see it peering down from one of the arches in Lincoln Cathedral) but the other escaped by throwing stones at the angel. I suppose it is one of these that missed and landed at Kinoulton.

EIGHT

IN THE GREENWOOD

We have now had several references to Sherwood Forest but only a passing mention of the iconic figure who springs to mind whenever Nottingham or Sherwood Forest are mentioned anywhere in the world – Robin Hood. Before we tell his story we have a couple of items with similar themes. The first concerns a gang of men who, in a way, emulated him.

THE RUFFORD PARK POACHERS

The plot for this story comes from a traditional English folk song which links two of my all time favourite singers: Joseph Taylor and Martin Carthy. Joseph Taylor, a beautiful singer, was an agricultural labourer from Saxby All Saints in Lincolnshire. Percy Grainger collected many songs from him in 1908 and recorded them on wax cylinders. Taylor had a pure, high voice and really knew how to deliver a lyric. Luckily those recordings have been reissued on vinyl and on CD so we can still appreciate him over one hundred years later. The Rufford Park Poachers was one the best from his repertoire of really good songs, although his most famous song was probably Brigg Fair, which was arranged for orchestra by the composer Frederick Delius. A story tells that Joseph Taylor was invited to the first performance (I'm not sure where it was, I seem to remember mention of a big hall in Beverley). There he was, all done up in his best Sunday suit and shiny boots, feeling lost in the sea of gentlefolk, but when the orchestra began to play he recognised the tune, said, 'That's my song' and stood up and sang it with the orchestra.

Martin Carthy has been one of the top names in the folk revival for over half a century, a great singer and guitarist and a lovely man. His version of Rufford Park is so good that very few other people have attempted it since.

Rufford Park itself, just off the A614 near Ollerton, is one of my favourite Nottinghamshire places and, over the years, I have done quite a lot of work there – storytelling, music, children's events. It was built as a monastery but with the Dissolution it became the home of the Talbot family. In 1626, it passed into the hands of Sir George Savile whose descendents continued to live there until the twentieth century, when it was bought by English Heritage. The events in this story happened in 1851.

The poor country folk of Nottinghamshire, indeed the poor country folk of most of England, were struggling to survive, to get enough to eat and to feed their families. The gentry were increasingly enclosing common land for their own personal use; fencing it off and refusing to let anyone else set foot on their estates. Perhaps it was fair enough for them to want sole right to kill the deer and pheasants which they had reared, but they also denied the people the ability to snare a wild rabbit or hare. Just being found on the land lead to gaol, transportation to Australia or, perhaps, even the death penalty, depending on the time of day, whether you were carrying a gun or traps, or if you happened to have a dead rabbit in your pocket. The owners employed 'gamekeepers' who were little different to private armies with orders to shoot on sight. They set mantraps which could permanently disable anyone unfortunate enough to set their foot in one, and they even set guns on posts with tripwires to set them off. If any modern dictator employed such methods to control his people he would be taken before the International Criminal Court for crimes against humanity. Little wonder then that poachers stopped venturing out alone and started going out in gangs. It was the only way they could face up to the gamekeepers.

Around Rufford Park that was the situation and the local men were getting desperate. They depended on those rabbits and the occasional pheasant, as had their fathers and grandfathers before them. Unless they went into the new factories in Nottingham there was little work going and that was poorly paid. The gamekeepers were becoming increasingly bold and bloodthirsty and nobody dared venture into the woods alone. So, in the year 1851 they decided to take action. They would teach the keepers a lesson; give them a taste of their own medicine.

A group of men got together and recruited their friends and other local people and one evening, they went 'mob handed' onto the Rufford Park estate, aiming to confront the keepers. It was rather like the mass trespass on Kinder Scout a hundred years later. They had their dogs and their snares, of which they set as many as possible, before the keepers found them. Then, armed only with sticks and stones, they faced up to the keepers

and the battle commenced. There were only ten keepers and they were soon overwhelmed and turned tail. Except, that is, for Roberts, the head keeper, who lay on the ground with a fractured skull caused by a large rock which had been thrown. He died at the scene. The poachers had won the battle but they didn't win the war for most of them had been recognised. The next day many of them were taken into custody. The four ringleaders were sent to trial and were sentenced to fourteen years' transportation to Australia. In reality this was a life sentence, for very few convicts were able to find the fare for a return passage even if they wanted to come back.

The Rufford Park poachers were amongst the last convicts sentenced to transportation, for the practice was abolished in 1867. In the seventy-nine years in which men, women and children were sent into permanent exile for often trifling misdemeanours, 160,000 convicts faced the journey to the Antipodes, a whole new continent was put on the map (coloured red of course) and the concept of Botany Bay entered the English psyche. There are still various hamlets or farms scattered around the countryside of England called Botany Bay – probably because they were cut off and miles from anywhere, including one near Retford.

Many people had sympathy for the poachers as the lyrics below illustrate. The Rufford Park Poachers is just one of very many powerful songs written and sung about both poaching and transportation:

A buck or doe, believe it so, a pheasant or a hare
Was set on earth for everyone quite equally to share
So poachers bold, as I unfold, keep up your gallant hearts
And think about those poachers bold, that night in Rufford Park.

THE KING AND THE MILLER
OF MANSFIELD

For the next story we go back to the time when Robin Hood is supposed to have lived. It is surprising that it has retained its identity and not been taken into the Robin Hood cannon. It comes from a ballad entitled 'A Pleasant Ballad of King Henry II and the Miller of Mansfield, &c.' which is in the Samuel Pepys collection.

The original ballad is in two parts and I have kept that form although, to my mind, the story is complete at the end of part 1. In live tellings that is where I would leave it.

> Henry, our royall king, would ride a hunting
> To the greene forest so pleasant and faire;
> To see the harts skipping, and dainty does tripping:
> Unto merry Sherwood his nobles repaire:
> Hawke and hound were unbound, all things prepar'd
> For the game, in the same, with good regard.

PART ONE

King Henry II was staying at Nottingham Castle. It was, officially, part of his Royal Progress around his kingdom to hear the views of his barons, to ensure that they were looking after his lands correctly and to supervise the collection of taxes. But that was just the official reason. The real, much more personal, reason was to enable him to spend a few days hunting in Sherwood Forest, for Henry was a keen huntsman and had been able to spend little time at his favourite sport recently.

It had been a fine, sunny, winter's day and Henry and his nobles had had a good day hunting; chasing bucks and does and killing several which they sent on ahead to Nottingham. When the day drew to a close the party dwindled, various knights went their own way and eventually, as dusk was falling, the King found himself alone in the forest; lost. He rode this way and that but could find no clue as to which way Nottingham lay, every road and track looked the same. He did not fancy spending a night alone in the forest, which could be a dangerous place.

At length he met a man coming along the road. He could tell by his garb that the man was a miller – it is not without reason that millers are often called 'Dusty'. He was walking briskly along the forest track and the King hailed him, asking the way to Nottingham.

'Stay back,' shouted the miller, swinging his staff. 'Don't come any closer. I do not believe that you would confront me in the forest for no reason.'

'What reason could I have for being here alone?' asked the King.

'You seem to me like some gentleman thief,' replied the miller, 'come to rob me of my hard-earned cash. I wager that you do not have a groat in your purse.'

The King laughed and assured the miller that he was no thief and that he did not need to rob him of his money for he had plenty of his own.

'What I am in need of though,' said the King, 'is directions to Nottingham or a bed for the night and I will pay you for it, even if it costs me forty pence,' and he offered the miller his hand.

'Nay, stay back,' said the miller. 'I would know you a lot better before I shake your hand. But you have an honest face so you may follow me back to my house where I will be able to see you better.'

So the King and the miller made their way through the forest until they came to his mill on the outskirts of Mansfield. When they entered the house it was full of smoke and steam and the smells of cooking. The King vowed that he had never been in so smoky a house before. When the miller had studied him in the light of the lamps he admitted that the King did seem to be an honest man and said that he could stay the night and share the room of his son, Richard.

The miller's wife urged her husband to beware. 'I admit he has a handsome face and a pleasant manner,' she muttered, 'but it's best to be wary.'

'Are you an outlaw?' she asked the king. 'If not, show me your passport and tell me the name of your master.'

'I have no passport,' replied the King, giving a low bow, 'and have never served a master. I am but a poor courtier who lost his way. But, I promise that everything you give me here I will repay you tenfold.'

The miller's wife whispered into her husband's ear, 'He is a comely youth and his speech and manners are good. I don't believe there is any danger in him staying here. It would be a sin to turn him out into the night.' And the miller agreed.

'Young man,' said the miller's wife, 'you may stay here and we will make you as comfortable as we can. In fact you can sleep with our son Richard. That is the very best we can offer you.'

Then the miller introduced himself as John Cockle, and he and the King shook hands. Fresh straw was fetched and put on the bed along with clean hempen sheets.

Richard was disappointed at having to share his bed with this strange young man. 'Are you clean?' he asked. 'Have you any creepers in your hose? Have you the scab or any other dirty diseases, because if you have you will not lie with me!'

This insolence did not offend the King but caused him to laugh 'til the tears rolled down his cheeks. He assured Richard that he was carrying no wildlife on his body and was suffering from no disease. Then the party sat down to a good meal: bag puddings followed by apple pies, all washed down with good, brown Nottingham ale. It was a merry meal with plenty of toasts. The miller drank to the visitor and he, in turn, proposed a toast to the boy, Richard. Then the miller's wife, feeling merry and wanting to impress their guest said, 'Hush, and I will fetch something special, something the like of which you will never have tasted before. She went to the pantry and brought back a large pasty. 'Taste of this sweetness,' she said.

The King ate and complimented the woman. 'What is it?' he asked, 'for I have never tasted its like before. It must be a very rare food and very expensive. I thank you for giving me such a rare treat.'

'Nay, not rare and not expensive,' laughed the miller. 'We eat it every day and pay not a penny for it, for we find it running wild on the hoof in the forest and fetch it home for free!'

'Then it must be the King's venison,' said the King in hushed tones.

'Oh, fool,' laughed the miller, 'of course it is. We are never without two or three fat deer hidden in the thatch. But keep that quiet. Do not say a word to anyone. We would not have the King know!' And he roared with laughter.

Henry promised that he would keep the secret and they all drank another toast: 'To the King! And to his deer!' and then retired to their beds where they all slept soundly.

When it was realised that the King had not returned to Nottingham his courtiers were frantic with worry and at first light the next morning they were up and out, searching for him in every town and village. They arrived at the miller's house just as the King came out to mount his horse. The terrified nobles immediately fell down on their knees and addressed the miller's guest as 'Your Majesty'. They begged his pardon that he had been left alone and had had to spend the night with the miller. To his horror the miller realised whom it was he had lodged for the night and he feared for his life. This fear was made worse when the King drew his sword. The miller fell on his knees expecting one blow to sever his head from his body but, instead, the King dubbed him a knight – Sir John Cockle – and gave him the land where his mill stood as his own. Then the King said his goodbyes to Sir John, and to his wife and to the Squire Richard, with whom he had shared his bed, and rode off, with his nobles, towards Nottingham.

PART TWO

Soon it was time for the King and his party to return to the court at Westminster. Later, when they were all assembled there, they began discussing the adventures and good times they had had on their journeys. The King said that he'd enjoyed much of it, but the time he had enjoyed most of all was the night he had spent with his new knight, Sir

John Cockle, the Miller of Mansfield. 'It is coming up to St George's Day,' he said, 'when we will again feast and make merry, and I would that good Sir John and his family were here to enjoy it with us.'

Messengers were sent north to greet the miller and to summon him to court. When they delivered their message the miller did not, at first, believe them. 'This is an odd jest,' he said, 'why would the King want us?'

'I expect we will all be hanged,' said Richard.

The messenger assured them that it was no trick and that the King really did want their company at the St George's Day celebrations, so the miller gave the man three farthings as a thanks for delivering the message and sent him back to London, with word that they would follow on with all haste and be there in time to join the King for the feast.

'Now,' said the miller, 'comes a time of great expense. We must be brave and buy what we need though it cost us all we have. We must all buy new clothes for we cannot go to London dressed in this country working gear. And we need horses and saddles and bridles, and servants fitting to our new status.'

'Nay,' answered his wife. 'You need spend no money on me for I will turn and trim my old russet gown and I will make your clothes and Richard's look as good as new. And don't fret about new horses for we will ride to London on our old mill horses and saddle them with flour sacks.'

And thus it was that the trio rode down to London with all the speed they could muster. Squire Richard rode in the front with a cock's feather stuck in his hat, Sir John trotted along behind and his wife brought up the rear, mincing along and looking for all the world like a farm worker playing the part of Maid Marian in the May Day revels.

The King, hearing of their coming, rode out to meet them and greeted them heartily. 'Well met, my old friend,' he said. 'And your good lady wife. And how do you do? And who is your noble Squire?'

'Do you not remember me?' asked Richard

'Of course I do. How could I forget my own bed fellow? He who tossed and turned all night long.'

'And how could I forget you?' replied Richard. 'You who made the bed hot with your farting.'

'Speak politely to your king,' blustered Sir John in worried tones.

But the King and his courtiers bellowed with laughter and he led his guests through the hall, past the court women and the ladies-in-waiting, who were all dressed up like the queens on a pack of playing cards, and he seated them at the table where a magnificent feast was served.

When the eating was finished, wine and beer were served and the King fell to joking. 'All this food and drink is very fine,' he said, 'but Madam, I would exchange it all for some of your "lightfoot" pasty.'

'Fie,' said Richard. 'Shame that you should eat it and then betray it. Hush yourself.'

'Why are you angry?' asked the King, 'I have drunk your health.'

'You drink our health but you feed us such piddling small amounts. What would I give for a black pudding,' said Richard.

'Aye, that would, indeed, be a fine thing if you could find one here,' replied the King, at which remark Richard reached into his hose and brought one forth, sweating from being carried in his breeches for so long. He fell on his knee and presented it to Henry.

After this the ladies prepared to dance and Sir John, his wife and Squire Richard attempted to join in but, being simple country folk and knowing none of the dances, their antics made the nobles laugh until their sides ached. When he could talk again, King Henry asked young Richard if there were any ladies there that he would like to wed. He replied that the red-haired woman called Jugg Grumball had promised to be his wife and the King granted their union.

Then the King called Sir John Cockle to him and made him the Overseer of merry Sherwood and granted him a pension of three hundred pounds a year on the condition that he steal no more deer and that he send the King a report once a quarter.

After that, King Henry bid them all adieu and sent them back to their home, where they lived out their lives in peace and prosperity and often reminisced about the time when the Miller of Mansfield gave hospitality to a gentleman thief who turned out to be the King.

NINE

THE STORY OF ROBIN HOOD

From wherever you are travelling, as you enter Nottinghamshire you see signs welcoming you to 'Robin Hood Country'. Mention Nottingham or Sherwood Forest anywhere in the world and people will know of Robin Hood. He is, arguably, England's number one hero. (Note, I said England's not Britain's, for then Arthur and others would come into the frame.)

The origins of the story of Robin Hood are lost in the mists of time. The first mentions of him come as early as 1363 and there are surviving manuscripts from soon after. The earliest of the stories are in ballad form. These ballads were written at different times over a period of perhaps five hundred years and the many different authors had different ideas about who Robin was, where he lived and at what period in history.

Many scholars have tried to make sense of them, to dig out 'the truth', and they have written long, long books identifying the 'real' Robin Hood and placing him in particular time frames. I have approached him in this retelling as a legendary figure – perhaps more fiction than fact – and I have concentrated on the fun and action, rather than the history and meaning. Robin accumulated all kinds of stories around his name; stories about other outlaws became Robin Hood stories just by changing the name. A ballad I have sung for many years is 'The Birth of Robin Hood', which finishes:

> And many a one sings of grass, of grass
> And many a one sings of corn,
> And many a one sings of bold Robin Hood
> Knows not where he was born.

> It was not in the hall, the hall
> Nor in the painted bower,
> But it was in the good green wood
> Among the lily flower.

It does not match the conventionally accepted story of Robin Hood for the simple reason that it wasn't originally written about Robin Hood. It was a Scottish ballad called 'Willie and Earl Richard's Daughter' but someone, at some time, changed the name. (I suspect it may have been Arthur Quiller-Couch in *The Oxford Book of Ballads*.)

Because of the vagueness concerning who he was and, particularly, *when* he was, certain discrepancies become apparent, for instance the name of the King. It is generally accepted in all the Hollywood/TV versions that Robin lived at the time when John was ruling in the name of Richard I, the Lionheart, while the latter was off fighting in the Holy Land or being held in captivity on his way home. John later became King in his own right. Both make an appearance here. But in some of the stories the King is named as Henry and his Queen Eleanor.

Henry could be any one of three kings, two of whom had queens called Eleanor. Richard and John were the sons of Henry II and Queen Eleanor of Aquitaine. Their older brother, Henry le Jeune Roy, was co-ruler with his father for several years, but his wife was Margaret of France. After Richard and John came John's son, Henry III and Queen Eleanor of Provence. The reigns of all these kings covered only a span of just over one hundred years so Robin could just about have lived through at least parts of them all, but I doubt it.

I have managed to keep some logic to the stories by having them spread over the reigns of the first two kings mentioned above – Henry II and Richard I, with John making a brief appearance as ruler in Richard's absence and King in his own right towards the end.

ROBIN BECOMES AN OUTLAW

The man whose reputation was to last for a thousand years and who was to become known world-wide as Robin Hood – the most famous outlaw of all time – was walking through the forest glades of Sherwood. He had been born and brought up within the forest and knew every inch of it, but now it all looked different. He saw things he hadn't seen before and he saw things he knew well with a different eye, for in the past few hours he had become a different person – not the son of a respected and important man, but a hunted man; prey for anyone who wanted to make a name for themselves or a few shillings for their purse; a wolf's head; an outlaw.

Robert Fitzooth, whom his friends sometimes called Robin of Lockesley after the place where he had been born, was the son of Hugh Fitzooth, the Head Forester of Sherwood and Barnesdale, a most important man who oversaw what happened in a huge area of forest in three counties. His power in the countryside was almost on a par with that of the Sheriff of Nottingham and Derby, who ruled over what happened in the towns. His father had taught Robin all he knew about forestry, archery and all kinds of woodland crafts, while his mother taught him to read, to dance and how to behave as a gentleman. This last aspect was fitting because some people believed that Fitzooth was the rightful Earl of Huntingdon and had been cheated out of that position, but whether that was the case or not, he was not interested in pursuing it. However, Fitzwalter (who was now the Earl) would have taken any opportunity to get Hugh and his son Robert out of the way to make his own position secure.

Robin had two particular friends with whom he would spend hours in the forest. One was his cousin, Will Gamewell, and the other was Marian Fitzwalter, daughter of Earl Fitzwalter who hated Robin's family so much. Robin and Marian had to be very clever and surreptitious about their friendship to keep it from Fitzwalter and his men.

Fitzwalter eventually saw his opportunity to get Hugh Fitzooth out of the way. Along with the Sheriff of Nottingham and the Bishop of Hereford, he whispered into the King's ear that his Head Forester was defrauding him and should be replaced (by another of their cronies of course) and it was done. Without warning, Hugh Fitzooth was arrested and taken off to Nottingham Castle, where he was held for months without charge and eventually died from neglect.

His wife and son were made homeless until they were taken in by Robin's uncle Gamewell. Robin's mother died as a result of the trauma and, to make matters worse, Will was now away at school and Marian had been sent off to the court of Queen Eleanor, the wife of King Henry II. Robin was left all alone. He spent his time in the forest learning every inch of its trackways and every hiding place there was to know. He also spent hours on end practising with his longbow until he was certain that there was no better archer anywhere to be found.

Then, one day, his uncle told Robin that there was to be an archery contest in Nottingham. The twelve best archers would be given employment as King's Foresters and the outright winner would receive a prize of a golden arrow. Robin couldn't wait to enter.

The day before the contest, as he walked through the forest on his way into Nottingham, Robin came upon a group of fifteen foresters drinking and feasting in a glade. They were merry and loud, very drunk and looking for trouble. Robin immediately recognised their leader as the man who had taken his father's place as Head Forester. They gathered round him and pushed him, asking him where he was going. When Robin told them they laughed and said, 'What a pretty little archer with a toy bow. What right do you have to shoot before the King and the Sheriff alongside all the proper archers?'

'I will bet you 20 marks that I can hit any target you care to name,' boasted Robin. The Head Forester pointed to a small group of deer which had just appeared from out of the undergrowth about 100 rods away.

'Hit me that hart,' he said, 'and you will be the best archer among us.' At that they all roared with laughter for to hit the hart at that distance would be a mighty shot. Without a second's hesitation Robin let fly an arrow. It flew true to its target and the deer leapt in the air and fell dead to the ground.

'The wager is mine,' said Robin and held out his hand for the money.

'Be off with you,' they yelled, 'before we kill you, for you have killed one of the King's deer and are now an outlaw.' Robin again drew his bow and before the drunken foresters could do anything, fourteen of the fifteen lay dead on the ground. The Head Forester squirmed on the ground and tried to hide but Robin found him, set him off running through the trees and then let fly an arrow which split his head in two. 'You said I was no archer,' said Robin. 'Your wives will now wish that I wasn't!'

And so that is how Robert Fitzooth, or Robin of Locksley, became an outlaw with a price on his head. But he was not yet Robin Hood and he had yet to find his 'merry men'.

THE ARCHERY CONTEST

After wandering randomly through the forest, Robin found himself at a place he knew well, the house of a poor widow. He had known her three sons for most of his life. She invited him in and gave him food and drink and lamented her woes. 'We live in hard times,' she said, 'it's not like it was in the past when we could take a deer or some pheasants and no one would mind as long as we kept quiet about it. The new Head Forester is a tyrant who comes down heavily on anyone who puts a toe out of line.' She told him that her sons had been made outlaws for killing deer to feed their families and they had gone off to join the many other young men who were hiding outside the law. Robin explained his situation and stayed with her until evening, when they came to visit their mother. They told Robin that there was a gang of them, fine men, but they needed someone to lead them, someone who could think ahead and plan as well as fight. They had decided that the one who could enter Nottingham and win the Sheriff's Golden Arrow would become their leader. 'That is perfect,' said Robin, 'for that was where I was heading when I was taken.'

The next morning, Robin disguised himself in old clothes with different coloured leggings and a hood to cover his head and set out for Nottingham. As he approached the town gates he saw notices offering a reward for 'The capture of Robert Fitzooth for the murdering of the King's loyal servant, the Head Forester'. Luckily the crowd was so dense that the soldiers at the gates didn't notice the young beggar-man slip past.

The archery contest was to take place in the afternoon and Robin lined up with the other contestants. There were twenty archers in all and Robin found himself alongside a large, swarthy man with one eye covered by a green bandage. Pavilions had been set up around the castle green and in them were the Sheriff, his wife and daughter, and their great friend the Bishop of Hereford. In a neighbouring pavilion Robin was surprised to see another young woman as well; one whom he had thought was in London. It was the Lady Marian alongside her father the Earl of Huntingdon. Robin was thrilled to be able to show his skill before such an audience. On the other side of the green crowded the populace of Nottingham, shouting for their favourites and hooting at the strangers, amongst whom were Robin and the man with the bandage.

The competition was to be held over three rounds. The first target was set at a distance of 30 ells. Those who missed the centre were eliminated. The next was 40 ells and those who made it to the final shot at 50 ells. Twelve of the archers made the second round and five the third. Robin, whom the spectators had nicknamed 'the beggar' and the man with bandaged eye, 'Blinder', seemed to have won over the crowd who were yelling for them, and they, in turn, appreciated each other's skill. They were determined to beat the remaining three archers, who were favourites of the Sheriff and his guests. In the final round these three shot first and, although their shots were good, they only just grazed the inner ring. Robin was to shoot next and as he stood with the bow drawn he glanced at the Sheriff's box and knew that he was shooting for the honour of his father. He let go the bowstring and the shot flew true to the dead centre. The crowd erupted. 'Beat that, "Blinder",' they yelled. The man with the green bandage stood solid, took aim, and let fly. His arrow grazed Robin's and landed just shy of the centre. 'Blinder' was the first to congratulate Robin as the winner. 'I hope we shall shoot together again,' he said. 'Now collect your prize with my blessing for I care nothing for it. I only wanted to win it to spite the Sheriff who is no friend of mine,' and with that he disappeared into the crowd.

Robin was led before the Sheriff who said, 'Despite your appearance you are a fine archer. Would you like to take service with me?'

'I am a free man,' replied Robin, 'and do not desire to serve anyone.'

The Sheriff swallowed his anger and presented Robin with the golden arrow. 'See that you bestow it wisely,' he said and the steward nudged Robin towards the Sheriff's daughter, who was waiting expectantly. But Robin walked to the neighbouring box and presented the arrow to Marian, who looked deep into his eyes. 'Thank you, Rob of the Hood,' she said, as the crowd cheered. Robin took the opportunity to slip away and headed for the town gate. He was off and on his way to Sherwood before the Sheriff's men had started searching for him.

That evening, he found the widow's three sons and the rest of their gang in the forest and told them what had occurred.

Some of them were loath to believe him until a man stepped out of the shadows. Robin recognised him as the archer with the green bandage, 'Blinder'. He vouched that everything Robin had said was true. He congratulated Rob of the Hood on his win and on upsetting the Sheriff by presenting the prize to the Lady Marian instead of the Sheriff's daughter. He introduced himself as Will Stutely and urged the men to accept Robin as their leader, which they were pleased to do. And so, in one day, Robin Hood won the Golden Arrow, his name and his gang of 'merry men'.

ROBIN HOOD AND LITTLE JOHN

For the rest of that summer, Robin and his men organised themselves and their way of life in the forest. Robin found he had, on the whole, a band of good men and any who failed to live up to the rules Robin laid down were soon sent away. The main rule was that they would never rob anyone who could not afford it and who did not deserve it, so the poor folk of the neighbourhood benefited from the outlaw's deeds. Anyone who fell on hard times and found themselves in great need would find a gift of food or money that would mysteriously arrive on their doorstep. In return, the outlaws were protected by the common folk. The only people who suffered and came to fear travelling through the forest were cruel noblemen and rich priests, who used the church funds to live a life of luxury. Robin was happy with his band but felt that he needed one more man, a man who could act as his lieutenant and take charge when he wasn't there.

One morning, Robin was walking around the edge of

the forest, visiting people and having a look around just to see what was going on. He came to a bridge across a small stream, just a tree trunk that had been laid across it. Usually he could have leaped across without bothering about the bridge but it had recently rained heavily and the stream had risen. Just as Robin set his foot on one end of the bridge a stranger did likewise on the other – a tall man, powerfully built, carrying a staff. 'Give way, man,' bawled Robin, 'or I'll teach you a lesson.'

'Ey up, youth,' said the stranger in a broad Derbyshire accent, 'you give way yoursel' or I'll have to teach you some manners.'

'Stand back,' yelled Robin, 'or I'll show you the way we do things in Nottinghamshire!'

'That's easy to say,' retorted the stranger, 'when you swagger there with your longbow and arrows while I have nothing but a staff.'

'Wait, don't move,' said Robin and he went off into the brush to cut himself a staff. Then the two men made their way to the centre of the bridge and the fight commenced. Robin was good with a quarter-staff but he was no match for the other man, who was not only a skilled fighter but was a head taller. After a few strokes either way, Robin suddenly found his legs whisked out from under him and he was toppling backwards into the stream.

He rose to the surface, blowing the water from his mouth and gasping for breath. The tall man jumped down onto the bank and offered his hand to pull Robin from the stream. When he was on dry land Robin put his horn to his lips and blew a loud blast and, after a few minutes, a band of men appeared from the undergrowth. Seeing what had happened they immediately wanted to give the stranger a good beating to teach him a lesson, but Robin stopped them. 'It was a fair fight,' he said, 'and I don't mind being defeated by a worthy opponent.' Then he asked the stranger his name and where he came from.

'My name is John Little,' he said, 'and I am a nailer from Hathersage in Derbyshire. And pray, what is your name?'

'You are a long way from home John Little,' said Robin. 'People call me Robin Hood and I am an outlaw in these woods.'

'Then you are the reason I have travelled so far,' said John Little. 'I have heard of you and decided to come and join your band, if you will have me.'

'That I will and right welcome,' said Robin.

And John Little was taken back to the outlaw's camp, where he was rechristened Little John and he soon became Robin's most trusted friend and companion.

ROBIN MEETS WILL SCARLET

The year rolled on and through the next winter Robin and his men took every opportunity to upset the Sheriff and to redistribute the wealth of any rich traveller who ventured into the forests of Sherwood or Barnesdale. When spring arrived again, Robin and Little John, who had become inseparable friends, happened to be strolling through Sherwood in the vicinity of the hamlet of Blidworth, not far from that bridge where they had first met, when they heard a man singing. They stepped off the path into the undergrowth to see who was coming. Soon a young man came sauntering along, singing a popular song as though he had not a care in the world. He was dressed from head to toe in scarlet – a scarlet doublet, scarlet silk hose and on his head a scarlet hat with a long, scarlet feather in it. The man's hair was long and golden and curled on his shoulders like a girl's; his step was light and skipping. He seemed the picture of a feckless, rich dandy. Little John, however, noticed what Robin didn't: that under his red cloak his shoulders were broad and the sword which hung at his side looked as though it was there for more than mere decoration.

'I'll warrant this young cock's purse holds more than it is right for him to carry through Sherwood,' said Robin. 'You stay there and I'll go and relieve him of some of the weight.' With that, Robin stepped out in front of the stranger and bid him to stop.

'Why should I stop?' he asked. 'Who are you? What is your name?'

'My name doesn't matter,' said Robin, 'but I am a tax-collector and I would like to lighten your purse a little.'

'You make me laugh,' chuckled the stranger. 'My purse holds no more money than I need and I do not intend to give it to you. Now step aside and let me be on my way,' and with that the stranger started on his way at the same steady pace he had been walking before.

By now, Robin was growing cross and he shouted that if the man did not stop he would bloody his head for him, and he swung his staff threateningly.

The stranger drew his sword and sighed 'Oh dear, and it was such a nice day up until now. I'm afraid I will have to run you through.'

'Put up your sword,' said Robin, 'for it will be broken at the first blow from my staff and it would be a pity to damage so fine a blade. Get yourself a staff and we will fight fairly.'

Little John was enjoying this encounter from behind a tree and was chuckling to himself. He was beginning to suspect that

Robin had underestimated this foe. His suspicion was reinforced when the man, instead of cutting a branch from a tree, went over to a small oak tree of the right size and with one tug pulled it from the ground. Then he trimmed the branches from it and faced up to Robin. The battle commenced and all three men were surprised at how it fell out. Little John was impressed by the fighting skill of both men; the man in scarlet received at least three blows which would have killed a lesser man; Robin was only hit twice but the second nearly finished the fight. At that point, Little John intervened and the scarlet stranger seemed ready to fight him as well but John assured him that there was no need.

Robin picked himself up from the ground: his hose were torn, his jerkin was covered in dust and he was bruised and bloody.

'You are a fine fighter and a noble gentleman,' said Robin. 'We will fight no more and you may go on your way unmolested by anyone in this forest. I am pleased to have met you.'

'If I am not mistaken,' said the stranger, 'you are Robin Hood, the famous outlaw who lives in these parts.'

'You are right,' replied Robin, 'but my fame has been tumbled in the dust today! May I ask what your name may be?'

'I am surprised that I did not recognise you immediately,' said the stranger, 'and that you do not know me, for I am your cousin and old playmate Will Gamewell!'

'Will Gamewell! My you've changed and grown into a fine man. I didn't recognise you but now I can see it. What brings you here? The last time I heard about you, you were in London. What news of your father and of the Lady Marian?'

Will Gamewell then told Robin how Marian was happy at the court of Queen Eleanor but still remembered their childhood days in the forest with great pleasure and how pleased she had been when 'Rob of the Hood' (whom she had recognised) had presented her with the golden arrow rather than giving it to the Sheriff's daughter. As for his father, he was in good health and was secretly proud of the way Robin was harassing the Sheriff. Then Will explained that he had been coming to find Robin in order to join his band for he too was now an outlaw; he had killed his father's steward who had been working against him on the Sheriff's orders.

They were all overjoyed to have Will Gamewell with them and, as they all went under aliases, they renamed him Will Scarlet. Will was a loyal member of Robin Hood's band and lived out his life in the area. His grave can still be found in the churchyard of St Mary's in Blidworth.

ROBIN MEETS FRIAR TUCK

In summer time, when leaves grow green,

And flowers are fresh and gay,

Robin Hood and his merry men

Were disposed to play.

Then some would leap, and some would run,

And some would use artillery:

'Which of you can a good bow draw,

A good archer to be?'

Robin Hood and his merry men had no love for churchmen. They thought the majority of them were corrupt and far from holy – they were probably not far wrong. They never hesitated to rob any bishop or prior who dared travel through the forest without many armed bodyguards. They had a particular dislike of the Bishop of Hereford, who was a great friend of the Sheriff of Nottingham, and they loved to ridicule him. On one occasion they caught him, made him feast on the King's deer, and then sent him back to Nottingham seated 'arse about face' on a donkey! But, if they heard of a churchman who was genuinely holy and cared for his parishioners in the proper manner, then they would do everything in their power to help him.

It was a lazy summer's day and the merry men were amusing themselves in the forest with sports and games. Little John killed a deer at five hundred paces and Robin congratulated him and said he would gladly travel a hundred miles to meet another archer who could match the shot.

Will Scarlet happened to hear this and said, 'I know of one. At Fountains Abbey there lives a curtall friar who would beat both of you.'

'Then I must go and visit that friar,' said Robin. 'I'll neither eat nor drink 'til I see whether your words are true.'

So Robin prepared himself. Under his jerkin of Lincoln green he put on a coat of chainmail and on his head a steel helmet. He took a sword and buckler, as well as his staff and longbow and set off to Yorkshire to seek out the friar. He supposed he might be more than just a fat holy man by his job, for a curtall friar was one who guarded the gates to an abbey – a medieval bouncer.

After a long, hot journey, Robin arrived on the banks of a wide river and sat himself down to rest. The river did not look too deep but he did not want to get his coat of mail wet and rusted so he looked up and down to find a way of crossing dry shod.

As he sat there he heard snatches of song coming from somewhere near at hand and then the sound of two voices engaged in argument. One was upholding the merits of hasty pudding but the other preferred a meat pie, especially

when flavoured with onions. After listening for a while, as the argument raged Robin became puzzled, for the two voices sounded so alike. And then the puzzle was answered, for through the bushes on the far bank came a fat, jovial-looking friar, holding in his hand a huge meat pie and talking to himself. He had a metal helmet on his head but otherwise he did not seem to be particularly warlike. The friar sat himself down on the opposite bank, removed his helmet, mopped his brow and proceeded to tuck into the pie, which rapidly diminished in size. Robin felt his mouth watering and thought he had better intervene before the pie vanished entirely so he stood up, fitted an arrow to his bow, and called out 'Hey, friar! Carry me over the water at once for I need to be on your side and I don't want to get my feet wet.'

As the friar stood up his cloak fell open to reveal a work-manlike sword hanging at his waist, but when he saw the arrow aimed in his direction he replied, 'Hold your hand and I will carry you over the water, for it is our duty in life to help one another.' The friar put down his pie and waded across the river to Robin, who climbed on his back and was piggy-backed safely over the water. When they reached the further shore Robin leapt nimbly down and picked up the pie. 'I am beholden to you, father,' he said.

The friar swiftly snatched up his sword and buckler and said, 'If you are beholden to me then now is your chance to repay the debt, for my business lies on the further shore. I see that you are an honourable man who would serve the Church so put down my pie and carry me back over the river.'

'But I shall wet my feet,' complained Robin.

'Are your feet more important than mine?' asked the friar. 'I already fear that I will get rheumatics!'

'I am not as strong as you,' said Robin. 'I cannot carry you with all your war gear, pray leave it on this side and I will carry you across.'

So the friar stripped off his sword, buckler and helmet and left them on the bank and Robin took him on his back and carried him back across the river. The water was deep and the current was strong; the stones on the riverbed were round and slippery and Robin had difficulty in keeping his feet with the friar's very substantial weight on his back. But the friar clung tightly to Robin's neck, gripped with his thighs and dug his heels in as though he were riding a war horse and eventually Robin managed to stumble ashore, where the friar dismounted. Before he could do another thing Robin drew his sword and held it at the friar's throat. 'You know what I want?' he said, 'to be on the other side of this river.'

So once more the friar took him on his back and stepped into the water. Robin was planning what he was going to do when they reached the other side, how he would overpower the friar so that he didn't have to carry him back again, when he suddenly felt himself slipping, and before he could do anything about it he found himself dunked in the water. He came up spluttering and clambered ashore. He found his bow and arrows and in fury let fly towards the friar. But the friar was a skilled warrior and he fended them all off with his buckler until Robin had none left. Robin was furious. He did not like being outfought and he liked even less being made to feel a fool. 'You psalm-singing hypocrite!' he yelled. 'Just you wait until I get you within reach of my sword,' and he plunged back into the river and made his way towards the friar who met him in mid-stream. Then they both set to with powerful, skilful strokes. They immediately realised that each was wearing chainmail, which their swords would not pierce, but before long both were bruised and breathless. As Robin lunged at the friar he felt his foot slip on a stone and he went down on his knees at his enemy's mercy, but the friar did not take advantage of Robin's mishap and waited for him to regain his footing.

'You are the fairest and best fighter I've met for many a day,' said Robin. 'Please will you grant me a boon? Let me blow three blasts on my horn before we commence fighting again.' And Robin put his horn to his lips and no sooner had he blown the three blasts then many men dressed in Lincoln green and carrying longbows came running out of the forest behind him.

'Please return the favour and allow me to whistle three blasts too,' said the friar, and he put his fingers to his lips and three piercing whistles rang through the woods. No sooner had he done so then a pack of fine hounds came leaping out of the trees towards him. Robin's men let fly their arrows at the hounds but they had been taught to evade them and when all the arrows had been fired they picked them up in their jaws and returned them to the bowmen.

'By the Lord,' gasped Little John, 'it is witchcraft and sorcery. I've never seen anything like it.'

And then Will Scarlet came up laughing at the farcical scene before him. 'Call off your dogs Friar Tuck,' he called, 'for this man is a friend. Introduce yourself.'

'Yes, I am Tuck,' said the friar. 'For seven years I have lived at Fountains Abbey and preached on Sundays and christened, married and buried the local people. And for all that time I have also guarded the gates and I have not yet met a man I would yield to, but you are a worthy fighter and I would feign know your name.'

'I am Robin Hood and I am very glad to know you for you are the reason I am travelling in these parts. Will told me about you and I set out to see whether what he said was right.'

'Then I beg you to forgive me. If I had known you were Robin Hood I would gladly have carried you across the river and shared my pie with you and asked nothing in return,' said the friar, grasping Robin's hand.

'Then come with us now,' said Robin, 'and live with us in the forest. We will build you a hermitage so that you can continue your preaching and also keep us on the straight and narrow path.'

And so Friar Tuck and Robin Hood crossed the river yet again, arm-in-arm this time, and the whole band returned to Sherwood.

ROBIN HOOD AND MAID MARIAN

For someone who was a brilliant archer, a doughty fighter with both sword and quarterstaff, a good leader, and generally a hero to both his men and all the common folk around – let alone a feared adversary of the Sheriff of Nottingham and the other noblemen and clergy he took against – it is surprising how many times Robin Hood let himself be made a fool of. He seems to have always been walking into situations he should have avoided and being beaten in fights he needn't have fought: we have already heard of the way he was beaten and fooled by Little John and Friar Tuck, for instance. Perhaps it was because he was basically a confident, optimistic man who was so 'at home in his skin' that he didn't mind if things went wrong as long as they weren't things that really mattered. When it did matter, if he was planning an assault on the Sheriff's stronghold at Nottingham, or rescuing some poor victim from a knight's dungeon for instance, then he planned carefully so that there was little chance of failure.

Robin Hood walked into one of those careless situations on the day he met Richard Partington, the page.

Robin had decided to go hunting and, as he did not know who he might meet, he disguised himself in old clothes and dirtied his face. He found himself strolling through parts of the wood he knew well from his youth and his thoughts turned, fondly, to those carefree days of playing with Will Gamewell and Lady Marian. Then he saw a fine hart across a glade and silently drew his bow but, before he could loose his arrow the deer fell dead, struck by another arrow from the other side of the glade. Then a young man, obviously a page, ran from the undergrowth carrying a bow. Robin stepped out from cover and spoke loudly: 'How dare you kill the King's deer, you stripling!'

'I have as much right to shoot the King's deer as the King himself,' said the youth proudly. There was something about the voice that seemed familiar to Robin but he couldn't place it.

'Who are you then, lad?'

'I'm no lad of yours and my name is my own,' replied the page drawing a sword and flying at Robin, who was forced to draw his own sword to defend himself. The youth had some clever tricks and had obviously been taught to fight properly, but he was small and light and Robin would have had no difficulty in defeating him very quickly if he had wanted to, but he didn't want to humiliate the lad so he allowed the fight to continue until the page was obviously tiring. Then Robin allowed the lad's sword to nick his wrist.

'Do you yield now?' asked the page and Robin agreed to call a halt.

'Now will you tell me to whom I owe this wound?' asked Robin.

'I am Richard Partington, page to Her Majesty Queen Eleanor, and I am in these woods seeking one Robin Hood.'

Again the voice troubled Robin. What was there about it? It was not the voice of a mature man and there was something soft about it. While he was speaking the youth was wiping his sword on a lace handkerchief and as he replaced it in his doublet it opened and Robin saw a gleam of gold – a golden arrow.

'Now I know you,' yelled Robin and took the page in his arms and kissed her, for it was his Marian in disguise. She had not recognised Robin through his disguise, but once she did she returned his sentiments. The two of them walked arm-in-arm back to Robin's camp, where she told him that she really had been seeking Robin with a message from the Queen, who had heard so many stories of Robin and his Merry Men. She wished to meet them, to see if the stories were true. With that in mind she had persuaded King Henry to make an amnesty so they could visit her in

London safely. So, a few days later Robin and four of his men went with Marian to London, where they were entertained by Queen Eleanor, who was duly impressed.

Whilst in London the outlaws took part in another archery contest in which they beat the King's finest bowmen, which angered the King greatly but, true to his word, he allowed them to return safely to Sherwood. However, about a month later the King sent word to the Sheriff of Nottingham that he wanted the outlaws of Sherwood Forest wiped out once and for all.

The Sheriff was delighted to have the opportunity to really hunt down and catch Robin Hood and he assembled every man he could to scour the woods. He had so many men at his back that he felt secure enough to venture into the forest himself. For days and weeks they hunted back and forth but saw no trace at all of any of the outlaws. The forest seemed to be empty. Angrily, he sat in Nottingham Castle wondering what else he could do . . . perhaps he needed to enlist yet more men, have an army enter the woods from the north whilst he came in from the south. In the end, his daughter intervened. She had hated Robin Hood ever since he had ignored her and presented the golden arrow to Marian Fitzwalter all those years ago. His humbling of her father only deepened this hatred. She decided that force was not going to find him. His trickery could only be brought down by even deeper trickery. Her first try was to recruit a tinker, a braggart called Middle, who was confident that he could find the outlaw. He did, but only to join the outlaw band himself.

The next recruit to her scheme was Arthur a-Bland, a tanner from Nottingham who was also a champion wrestler, but he also failed to deliver Robin to the Sheriff, for he was a kinsman of Little John and merely joined them for a feast of venison in the outlaw camp, before he too stayed on to become another of the band, which had by this time grown to well over one hundred men.

All kinds of other tricks and traps were tried but none were successful. With the help of the poor people of Sherwood and some of the inhabitants of Nottingham, Robin was always aware of the Sheriff's plans and managed to stay one jump ahead.

Robin and the 'merry men' lived for over a decade in the fastnesses of Sherwood Forest. Sometimes there were long spells of peace when the men could creep quietly back to their homes and families and could live almost like any of the other cottagers in the neighbourhood. But then trouble would erupt again and they would return to their lives of outlawry.

They also travelled. They once took refuge in a small fishing village hidden away at the bottom of cliffs in a remote bay in Yorkshire. When things became too hot in Sherwood they would move en-masse to the forests of Barnesdale in Yorkshire, or remote, wild Longdendale in the north of Derbyshire. Throughout all this time the gang acted as a counter-balance to the authorities, redistributing the fines and taxes levied by greedy churchmen or the Sheriff of Nottingham. With the aid of friendly nobles, like the honourable Sir Richard of the Lea, they carried out an endless guerrilla war against Sir Guy of Gisbourne and Prince John, who was not so much evil as absolutely selfish.

Time passed and King Henry died to be succeeded by King Richard, known as the Lionheart. Richard would have been a good king but his interest lay not in England but in the wars against Saladin and his Muslim troops in the Holy Land. He immediately left on a crusade, leaving his brother, John, to look after his interests in England. But John looked after his own interests. He used the opportunity to put his own men into positions of power and to take what he wanted for his own use. One of the things he cast his eye on was Queen Eleanor's page, Richard of Partington, otherwise known as Maid Marian.

One day, Robin was in the forest when he was unexpectedly charged by a huge stag. He only managed to escape by jumping behind a tree. The stag turned and charged again, this time at a figure which had just emerged from behind some bushes on the other side of the clearing. To his horror Robin saw that it was Marian. She leaped out of the way but the stag's antlers caught her; a glancing blow that knocked her to the ground. She lay there, stunned. As the stag was preparing to gore her Robin managed to kill it with an arrow to the centre of its forehead. To his relief he found that Marian was not badly hurt and she told him how Prince John had tried to carry her away to one of his castles, so she had fled to join Robin in the wood. He took her back to the outlaw camp where, to the joy of the outlaw band, she became their newest recruit. Most of the other outlaws had taken aliases and Marian spent part of her time as Richard Partington but at other times, particularly when she was alone with Robin, she put on female clothes and became Maid Marian.

ROBIN HOOD AND THE KING

One wet windy evening, Friar Tuck was snuggled in the warmth of his hermitage with a flagon of mulled wine and a steaming venison pie when the dogs began to bark. A stranger was approaching. 'Who would come here disturbing me on a night like this?' he growled, hoping the traveller would pass by. But then there came a knocking at the door. 'Go away,' he yelled. 'You will get no lodging here. Go on to Gamewell, it's only a few miles.'

'It might be "only a few miles" if you know the way,' came a deep voice from outside, 'but I don't and I don't fancy wandering round this dismal forest for the rest of the night. Open the door and let me in, for I'm wet without and dry within.'

'How dare you disturb a holy man at his prayers,' muttered Tuck as he picked up his staff and opened the door. Outside stood a knight clad in black armour with a black plume in his helmet. By his side stood his horse, also richly clad.

'I must beg food and drink for myself and my steed, and a bed for the night,' he said.

'I fear I have nothing that your horse would fancy let alone a knight of your status,' replied Tuck.

'Nonsense, I can smell a tasty meal from here outside the door. Just let me tie my horse at the sheltered side of the house and I will come and test its worth. And I assure you that I will pay you well – either in gold or in blows, it is your choice.'

Tuck went to tie the horse in the lea of the house and gave it some hay while the knight strode into the house. When Tuck returned he had taken off his helmet and he saw he was a strong, brown-skinned man of middle age with blue eyes and a long beard tinged with gold. Although he looked strong and proud there was something pleasant about his appearance and Tuck immediately warmed to him.

For the rest of the evening the two men talked as they feasted. The knight seemed to have been everywhere and had had all kinds of adventures. He had been on pilgrimages and crusades; he had fought Saladin in the Holy Land, been imprisoned and escaped; he had both killed and been injured in battle but he laughed it all off as though it was not important. They talked and swapped yarns until they both fell asleep with their heads on the table among their dishes.

In the morning, Tuck awoke to find the knight already up and preparing gruel for breakfast. He refused to take any payment for his hospitality but said he would willingly help the knight on his way however he could.

'Well then,' said the knight, 'I would like to meet an outlaw of these parts who goes by the name of Robin Hood. Can to tell me where I can find him?'

Tuck feigned horror: 'Sir,' he said, 'I am an honourable holy man. How can you imagine that I know anything about such an outlaw?'

'I mean him no harm,' said the knight. 'I have heard much about him and I would like to meet him to see if, in the flesh, he lives up to the stories.'

'Well, you cannot live in these parts without hearing something of Hood,' admitted the friar. 'I might be able to take you to a place where you just might find him.'

And so the pair set off, the knight riding grandly on his charger and the friar striding along beside him. After they had been a few miles a man suddenly stepped out of the undergrowth and bid them stop. 'I am the guardian of this highway,' he said, 'and must extract a toll from all who travel it.'

'I am not in the habit of yielding to any one man,' said the knight.

'Then see that I am not alone,' said Robin Hood, for that is, of course, who it was, and several more of his men joined him.

'We are messengers of the King,' said the knight. 'King Richard himself is staying nearby and he sent me to seek out one Robin Hood whom he would like to meet.'

At that Robin removed his hat and bowed low. 'God save the King!' he said. 'We are loyal servants of His Majesty. We have no argument with him. Our fight is with rich and greedy nobles and clergy who take what is not theirs. If we do anything against the King's laws it is only to take a few deer to sustain ourselves.'

Then the knight was taken back to the outlaw's camp where everyone was assembled and a great feast given. The King was toasted many times during the meal and then the games began: there was wrestling and games of skill, fighting demonstrations with swords and staffs and, last of all, an archery contest. The knight watched with increasing admiration.

When night came on he was made comfortable in a forest hut.

The outlaws were woken in the morning by the sound of mounted men and they rushed out with their weapons ready to protect themselves but it was only a friendly knight, Sir Richard of the Lea, with his men. As soon as Sir Richard saw the knight in the black armour he leaped from his horse and fell to his knees. 'Your Majesty,' he said, and everyone realised who the strange knight was, it was none other than the King himself, King Richard I, the Lionheart. Robin and his men cast aside their weapons and fell to their knees. 'Forgive us Sire,' said Robin, 'for we had no idea who you were.'

Then the King said, 'Last night you assured me that you were all outlaws through no choice of your own and that you would all be good servants to the King if you were able. Is that still the case?'

The outlaws, with one voice, said it was.

'Then here and now I pardon you all and take you all into my service,' said the King. 'I cannot allow such archers as you

to roam my forests killing my deer, but I can think of various treacherous nobles who I could use you against.'

So King Richard made the outlaws Royal Foresters, to protect the forests. Little John was made Sheriff of Nottingham.

'And I hope you do the job better than the man you follow,' said the King, 'although that would not be difficult.'

The King then called to the rest of Robin's men, who he pardoned and gave positions at court and reinstated their lands. 'There is a lot to do in this country of ours,' he said. 'The laws and taxes have been warped so that they weigh unfairly on the poor and needy who cannot afford to pay them, while the rich and powerful are given carte blanche to do and take what they want! We have to return England to the fair and honest land it once was and I need men like you to help me.'

Finally the King called to Robin. 'Did you not once have a sweetheart at court?' he asked. 'Pray, what has become of her? You haven't forgotten her?'

At that the page came forward and bowed low in a courtly fashion. 'Indeed he has not, Sire, for I am here.'

'And so you are. And are you not the daughter of the Earl of Huntingdon?'

'Indeed I am, Sire, although some would say that Robin is the rightful Earl,' replied Marian.

'Then in that case I will make him Earl again – in fact I will grant you both the Earldom jointly in case you revive the ancient quarrel.' With that, the King touched Robin on the shoulder with his sword. 'Arise Robin Fitzooth, Earl of Huntingdon,' he said. 'And my first command to my new earl is that you take this woman and marry her as soon as possible.'

That night, Robin and his men, along with the King, slept out under the stars and in the morning they rose and made their way towards Nottingham.

At the head rode King Richard, the Lionheart, in his black armour and the black plume in his helmet; followed by Sir Richard of the Lea, with fourscore knights and men-at-arms, followed by Robin Hood and Maid Marian riding upon milk-white steeds. They were followed by seven score of Robin's archers, clad in Lincoln green with their bows unstrung in token of peace. They entered the city to the cheers of the populace and made their way to the castle, where they were greeted by the Sheriff and the Bishop of Hereford, along with several other noblemen. King Richard ordered the Sheriff to hand over the keys to Little John and to leave the city immediately. He warned the Bishop that he had many crimes to answer for and restitution to make for all the lands he had taken unlawfully, but first he had a wedding to perform, that of Robin Hood and Maid Marian.

THE DEATH OF ROBIN HOOD

For the next few months King Richard, accompanied by his Royal Archers, travelled throughout England righting the wrongs which had occurred in his time away. Then the King returned to London; Robin and Marian went with him. Half of the archers accompanied them and the other half went to Sherwood to look after the King's lands there. Marian was accustomed to life at court and soon became one of the most fashionable of courtiers but Robin did not like the restrictions, he longed for the freedom of the forest. Eventually he asked leave to travel and the King sent him on various errands in foreign lands. Robin took Marian with him and they travelled far and wide until, in some eastern land, Marian caught the plague and died. They had been married for a mere five years and Robin was heartbroken. He returned to England to find that King Richard was off crusading again and Prince John was once more in charge. He immediately had Robin locked up in the Tower, from where he was freed by his merry men and escaped to Sherwood.

Eventually, the news reached Robin that King Richard was dead and John was now King in his own right. This was bad news indeed. One day Little John arrived at the outlaw's camp. 'Have you come to arrest us?' called Robin.

'No, I am no longer the Sheriff,' replied Little John. 'The new king has replaced me and I'm not sorry for it for I have longed to rejoin you here.'

After that, King John waged a relentless war on the outlaws, so much so that they fled from Sherwood and Barnesdale and went into Derbyshire, where they found refuge near Haddon Hall at a place where there are caves in the rocks – it is still called Robin Hood's Castle or Robin Hood's Stride. But they were followed there too and eventually Robin was wounded in a battle and, probably because he was sad and depressed as well as older, he did not heal as quickly or as well as he had done in the past. 'I fear our days are numbered,' he said to Little John. 'Never again will we have the adventures and fun we enjoyed in the past. I will go to a cousin of mine, a nun at Kirkley Hall, and see if she will bleed me so that I can regain my energy.'

Little John bid Robin farewell and hoped that there would be good news to exchange when next they met. Robin made his way to Kirkley Hall in Yorkshire and by the time he arrived he was exhausted. He knocked on the door and his cousin let him in and, seeing his condition, insisted on blooding him straight away. Robin lay on a bed while the nun opened a vein and as the blood dripped he dropped off to sleep. Several hours later he awoke and immediately realised that he had been betrayed. He was still bleeding and he had lost so much blood that he could hardly rise from the bed. He staggered to the window, put his horn to his lips, and blew three feeble blasts. Little John, who had followed him and was hiding close by, heard the horn and realised from the sound that Robin was in trouble. He ran to the hall, burst open the door and rushed up to the room where Robin was. When he saw that Robin was dying he was all for burning down the building and killing all the inhabitants there and then, but Robin stopped him. 'Never in my life have I burned any holy building or harmed any nun or woman of any kind so I will not start now,' he said. 'Just fetch me my bow and let me shoot one final shot. Where the arrow lands there I will be buried.'

So Little John supported Robin as he stood at the window and drew back his bow. He summoned up all his strength and let fly one last arrow which flew a prodigious distance. Then he fell back into John's arms, dead.

The remaining Merry Men were summoned and Robin was buried where his arrow had fallen. A stone was carved to mark the spot. On it was written these words:

Underneath this little stone
Lies Robert, Earl of Huntingdon.
No archer was like him so good
His wildness named him Robin Hood.

TEN

NOTTINGHAM CASTLE

THE LEGEND OF MORTIMER'S HOLE

If you visit Nottingham you'll almost certainly see the statue of Robin Hood standing below the Castle Rock (and it will probably be complete, although at one time it was a regular occurrence for his arrow to be stolen) and you may well take a guided tour of Mortimer's Hole, a tunnel over 100 metres long, starting in Brewhouse Yard and stretching underneath and up into the castle grounds. At one time it was high on the 'to do' list of most visitors to Nottingham. Tourists of all

kinds, whether Victorian ladies or 1950s schoolboys, would be taken through the tunnel and told the story of how it was used to sneak soldiers into the castle to capture a tyrant who was attempting to take the crown of England. It could be a fictional tale, like Robin Hood, but it is a true story about kings and queens and the machinations of state. It reads like a fairy tale but it is a slice of real British history from the fourteenth century.

Queen Isabella was the wife of King Edward II but she didn't love him. No, Queen Isabella loved a young man called Roger de Mortimer. Between them, Isabella and Mortimer plotted the death of Edward II and succeeded in bringing it about. Edward's son became King Edward III but as he was still only a child his mother ruled for him as regent. She promoted her lover, Mortimer, and made him Earl of March, giving them the ability to do whatever they wanted. Together they set up home in Nottingham Castle and ruled the country from there, riding out and looting the countryside and defying anyone and everyone, whatever their rank. In the end, they had the King's uncle, the Earl of Kent, killed for no better reason than because they could. It was also to warn any of the other nobles not to stand up to them. However, this move proved to be their undoing. It was a step too far. The other nobles of the country decided that something had to be done to remove the two tyrants and to put the young king, who was by now eighteen years old and able to rule in his own right, onto the throne.

Isabella and Mortimer were at Nottingham Castle, guarded by about 180 knights. The castle, perched on its rock above the town, was impregnable and the pair were obviously frightened of being betrayed, because every night the gates were locked and Isabella slept with the keys under her pillow.

Parliament assembled in Nottingham and Edward III and his wife, Queen Philippa, also came to Nottingham and a plan was formed. The man behind the plan was Sir William Mountacute. He spoke to the constable of the castle, Sir William Elland, and won him over. Elland knew every inch of the castle, including a secret tunnel under the walls, and he agreed to lead a party to capture Mortimer, who was the main target. One night, the party slipped through the tunnel into a chamber adjoining Isabella's bedchamber. There they found Mortimer, and after a brief tussle in which several of his supporters were killed, he was placed under arrest. Mortimer was hustled back out via the same passage by which his captors had entered. This was all achieved so quickly and quietly that the soldiers guarding the ramparts were unaware that anything had happened.

The next day Mortimer's sons and supporters were rounded up and arrested and the people of Nottingham learned that there was a new regime in charge.

Mortimer was taken to the Tower of London and parliament was assembled in Westminster. They convicted Mortimer of high treason and on 30 November 1330, he was drawn and hanged on a common gallows. His body was allowed to hang on display for two days, after which it was interred in the church of Greyfriars.

The story of the sneak attack on the castle proved very popular and the tunnel became known as Mortimer's Hole. Seven hundred years later, it is still a tourist attraction and visitors to Nottingham enjoy the dark climb through the tunnel and the exciting story which goes with it.

The tunnel they are shown, though, is probably not the one which was used for these events. It is probably just a service tunnel into the castle from the River Leen, which ran around the bottom of the Castle Rock. What is believed to be the 'real' Mortimer's Hole has recently been discovered and excavated by local archaeologists, its entrance is further off in the garden of a house in the area now known as The Park – not at the base of the cliffs.

THE TRIP TO JERUSALEM

There are all kinds of other tunnels and caves in the Castle Rock too, some natural and some man-made, for it is quite soft sandstone. There used to be a whole class of workers in Nottingham known as 'sandmen' whose job was to dig the sand and sell it to housewives, who would use it to clean their floors and scour their pots and pans. A by-product of this was huge caves, but some of the caves are much older. Way back in pre-Roman times the local Britons, the Coritani, called the site now occupied by the castle, Tigguocabauc, 'the house of caves'. It was not a major settlement, in fact they may not have even lived there permanently but they did, definitely, use the caves and over the years since then many of them have been linked by passages. Those of you who have sat listening to songs or stories, or perhaps just having a quiet drink in the Rock Lounge at Ye Olde Trip to Jerusalem public house, which is partly built into the cliff, will have experienced the sand dropping down into your beer and will know, first hand, just how soft the rock is in places. Just round the corner from the Trip is Brewhouse Yard, but it seems likely that the Trip started life as the brewery for the castle.

Nottingham has long been famous for brewing. There are now several small breweries in the city and the oldest, The Nottingham Brewery Co., dates back to at least 1847, when it was famous for exporting its India Pale Ale to Britons serving in India. Nottingham University offers a degree in Brewing Science. None of this is surprising because back in the seventeenth century Daniel Defoe commented on the great crops of barley grown in the Trent Valley. Burton-on-Trent, which is only a few miles away, became the commercial brewing centre but Nottingham Ale was the one which warranted a song.

> When Venus, the goddess of beauty and love
> Arose from the froth that swam on the sea
> Minerva sprang out of the cranium of Jove
> A coy, sullen dame as most mortals agree;
> But Bacchus, they tell us, that prince of good fellows
> Was Jupiter's son, pray attend my tale,
> They who thus chatter mistake quite the matter
> He sprang from a barrel of Nottingham Ale.

> Chorus:
> Nottingham Ale, me boys, Nottingham Ale
> No liquor on earth is like Nottingham Ale
> Nottingham Ale, me boys, Nottingham Ale
> No liquor on earth is like Nottingham Ale

This is the first verse of a song which was very popular in the city's folk clubs twenty or thirty years ago. It is by an anonymous writer.

Ye Olde Trip to Jerusalem claims to be the oldest pub in Britain, dating back to 1189. The name is said to have come from the fact that the knights of Richard the Lionheart stopped there on their crusades to the Holy Land. (But if they had started from the castle, they hadn't gone far!) However much of that is truth and however much is legend, it is, without doubt, a picturesque, atmospheric place to have a drink. Twenty years ago it was 'rougher', more natural. Now it is a bit like a museum with exhibits in glass cases. One of these exhibits is a cobweb-shrouded sailing ship. It is now behind glass but it used to hang from the ceiling in the rock lounge. The reason it is still 'cobweb shrouded' is that no one dares clean it. It is said that anyone who tries will die a sudden and mysterious death! Several people have tried and they have!

ELEVEN

THE ENDLESS TALE

Tales can be seen as endless and immortal – they go on for ever, being handed down from generation to generation and changing as they go; sometimes growing, sometimes shrinking but, as another of my stories says, 'they never wear out'. We shall finish with one which could, literally, last for ever in more ways than one. If Scheherazade had started with it, the *Arabian Nights* might have been one thousand tales shorter.

Once upon a time, there was a king who had a very beautiful daughter. She was so beautiful that many princes wished to marry her and the King did not know how to decide which one to choose. In the end, he decided that he should set a test; the princess would marry the man who could tell him a tale that had no end. However, if they failed to tell an endless tale they would be beheaded.

Despite the threat, many young men came and tried to tell an endless tale, but all the stories somehow came to an end, so they were beheaded.

One day, a poor traveller who happened to be passing through the kingdom heard of the test and thought he would like to marry a princess. He decided he would try his luck.

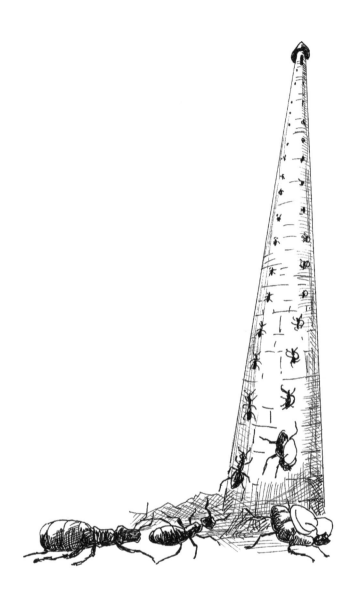

The King sighed and agreed to listen, and the traveller began:

'Once upon a time a man built a huge barn. It covered many acres and reached almost to the sky. He left just one tiny hole at the top through which there was only room for one ant to creep in at a time. When it was finished he filled the barn full of corn to the very top. When he had filled the barn an ant went in through the hole at the top and fetched one grain of corn and took it back to its nest, and then another ant came and fetched another grain of corn and took it back to its nest, and then another ant came and fetched another grain of corn and took it back to its nest, and then another ant came and fetched another grain of corn and took it back to its nest, and then another ant came . . . '

The traveller continued, saying, 'And then another ant came and fetched another grain of corn and took it back to its nest . . . ' for a long, long time.

In the end, the King grew so weary and bored that he shouted to the traveller to stop. 'Alright,' he said. 'The tale is endless. You have passed the test and can marry my daughter!'

So he did.

BIBLIOGRAPHY

Main Sources

Addy, Sidney Oldall, *Household Tales & Traditional Remains: Collected in the Counties of York, Lincoln, Derby & Nottingham* (David Nutt, The Strand, London, and Pawson & Brailsford, Sheffield, 1895)

Briscoe, John Potter, *Stories About the Midlands, being a collection of anecdotes relating to Nottinghamshire, Derbyshire, Lincolnshire and Leicestershire,* (Hamilton, Adams & Co., London, and Joseph Derby, Nottingham, 1883)

Briscoe, John Potter, *Nottinghamshire Facts & Fictions*, (a series of booklets published in the 1870s and 1880s, available at Nottingham Local Studies Library)

Jewitt, Llewellyn, *The Ballads & Songs of Derbyshire* (Bemrose & Sons, Derby, 1867)

Other Collections

Briggs, Katherine M., *Dictionary of British Folk Tales* (Routledge & Kegan Paul Ltd, 1970)

Briggs, Katherine M. and Ruth L. Tongue (ed.*)* *Folktales of England* (Routledge & Kegan Paul Ltd, 1965)

Bronson, Bertrand Harris, *The Singing Tradition of Child's Popular Ballads* (Princeton University Press, 1976)

Child, Francis James, *The English and Scottish Popular Ballads* (1888)

Defoe, Daniel, *A Tour Through the Whole Island of Great Britain* (Penguin, 1971)

Haslam, David, *Ghosts & Legends of Nottinghamshire* (Countryside Books, Newbury, 1996)

Howat, Polly, *Tales of Old Nottinghamshire* (Countryside Books, Newbury, 1991)

Jacobs, Joseph, *More English Fairy Tales* (David Nutt, The Strand, London, 1894)

Mayfield, Pat, *Legends of Nottinghamshire* (Dalesman Books, 1976)

McSpadden, Walker, *Robin Hood* (Project Gutenberg, 1891)

Palmer, Roy (ed.) *Folk Songs Collected by Ralph Vaughan Williams* (Dent, 1983)

Robb, Rosemary, *Ghosts and Legends of Newark* (J.H. Hall & Sons, Nottinghamshire Heritage Series, 1989)

Swift, Eric, *Folk Tales of the East Midlands* (Thomas Nelson & Sons Ltd, 1954)

Trease, Geoffrey, *Nottingham: A Biography* (Macmillan, 1970)

Westwood, Jennifer and Jacqueline Simpson, *The Lore of the Land* (Penguin, 2005)

Recordings (CDs)

Castle, Pete, *The Jenny & the Frame & the Mule* (MATS023, includes 'Edward Pepper')

Castle, Pete, *Mearcstapa* (MATS022, includes 'The Birth of Robin Hood')

Both available from Pete's website: www.petecastle.co.uk

ABOUT THE AUTHOR

PETE CASTLE has been a professional folk singer and storyteller for well over thirty years. He first became really interested in the folk tradition when he lived in Nottingham in the 1970s, although he'd been playing music since he was at school. He now lives in Derbyshire.

Pete has performed all over the UK at folk clubs, concerts, and festivals as well as doing work in schools, libraries, and heritage sites. They range from tiny local community groups to the largest festivals. He highlights the Smithsonian Folklife festival in Washington DC, where he was invited to perform in 2007 alongside hugely talented performers from Virginia and West Africa. That festival claims audiences of well over a million people every year!

As well as performing, he has run workshops for organisations as varied as the Workers Education Association, The Workers Music Association, Avril Dankworth Youth Music Camps and many local authorities.

Pete also edits *Facts & Fiction*, the UK's only storytelling magazine, and is the author of *Derbyshire Folk Tales*.

If you enjoyed this book, you may also be interested in ...

Derbyshire Folk Tales

Pete Castle

Passed down from generation to generation, many of Derbyshi
most popular folk tales are gathered together here for the first
time. Richly illustrated with original drawings, accounts of love
loss, heroes and villains are all brought to life through vivid
descriptions that have survived for several centuries.

978 0 7524 5388 0

Shropshire Folk Tales

Amy Douglas

The thirty stories in this collection have grown out of the
county's diverse landscapes: tales of the strange and macabre;
memories of magic and other worlds; proud recollections of
folk history. These traditional tales are full of Shropshire wit a
wisdom, and will be enjoyed time and again.

978 0 7524 5155 8

Highland Folk Tales

Bob Pegg

In a vivid journey through the Highland landscape, from
towns and villages to the remotest places, by mountains, cl
peatland and glen, storyteller and folklorist Bob Pegg takes
reader along old and new roads to places where legend and la
scape are inseparably linked.

978 0 7524 6090 1